From the World of Business

If you would like to lead a well-organized professional and personal life, this book is a must-read. I didn't realize how much of my mind and brain I was leaving out of my daily life. I learned a lot from these principles. They helped me understand the power I have to shape my world from within and to decide how open and creative I can be.

Jerome Peribere, President and CEO Scaled Air

Sharing these principles with thousands of people in our company improved our performance so dramatically that we shattered our commitments and objectives year after year. The more deeply our workforce understood and moved in the direction of what the authors are pointing to, the more resilient and successful we became. This understanding became our single most important competitive advantage and a primary factor in our success.

Ken, Robin, and Sandy have done a wonderful job capturing the power and the elegant simplicity of these principles and, in doing so, have done the world an enormous favor.

Read this book. Absorb its message. Let it lead you to your own insights and help you to unleash the power of the principles for yourself.

This book may help transform your business … and it may just change your life.

Don Donovan, Former Aerospace and Defense Executive President and Board Member Three Principles Global Community, LLC

The insights shared in this book helped me and my team better trust the innate wisdom in ourselves and in each other. Our relationships and business processes became more pure and our results greatly improved.

Jerry Bellis, President Titleist

Capturing this wisdom in a book is an extraordinary accomplishment. *Invisible Power* describes many challenging circumstances of being human and helps look at them from a different perspective. This book is straight, simple, deep, and relaxing to the busy mind. I got creative ideas that changed the way I look at difficult problems. I'd like to cite one of the book's many powerful sentences:, "Whether you realize it or not, ALL of your experiences, feelings states, and realities derive from a creative process happening inside your own mind."

Thanks to Ken, Robin, and Sandy for having refreshed and inspired me in such a meaningful way. I'm recommending it to everyone.

Luca Mantovani, Executive Vice President – Board Member Olon Spa – Infa Spa

By realizing how the mind works, I am able to spend much more time in a balanced state, allowing deeper capacities to be more fully on line. I am quicker to engage in clearing hurdles as they arise. I have more capacity to get work done with less effort, solve complex issues quickly, hear what is being said more deeply, and be more alert and connected with others. Overall, it has been a great source of relief to know that this is all built in, if only we know where and how to look.

Jim Collins, Executive Vice President DuPont

This book will change the way you think about the world, about yourself, and about other people. It is about who we are as human beings, how we think, and how we access the resources to solve seemingly intractable problems by tapping our innate intelligence. If we absorb its insights, this book teaches us to think with our entire souls, makes us better and more authentic leaders, and enables us to generate profound, concrete business results.

Michael Gordon, Chief Executive Officer Lombard International

I was introduced to insight principles more than a decade ago. As a result, I have witnessed tremendous transformations in individuals and teams in my organization, leading to much higher effectiveness and business performance. The principles have greatly impacted me both professionally and privately. This book now makes these principles available to a much broader audience. I recommend it to anyone who wants to achieve a calm mind, transformational results, and rewarding relationships in today's increasingly complex and pressured business environment.

Stephan B. Tanda, Executive Managing Board Director Royal DSM

An understanding of insight principles has helped our people to become better leaders, team players, and individuals, which significantly benefited our business results. We also saw improvement in our work environment and culture and these benefits spilled over to our personal lives. We came to realize that being present in the moment and being aware of our state of mind are two critical elements of effective leadership. What a profound impact this has had on the way our leaders serve their teams. *Invisible Power* contains the knowledge you need to get these results and more. You should read it.

Antonio Galindez, CEO (retired) Dow AgroSciences

If you are looking for an operating manual for the human mind—this book is it. Realizing insight principles has transformed the way my team and I approach and think through problems. We get to clarity quicker, expediting decision making and optimizing the results.

Paula Tolliver, Corporate Vice President and CIO Intel Corporation

My work with this understanding has had considerable impact for me personally and for my teams. The biggest benefit for me personally has been the deep insights that have helped me get my own state of mind and inner wisdom in order. This has helped to drive and inspire my people and the organization and helped to achieve the organization's hard objectives. I realized that sometimes our thoughts got in the way of good business performance and effective communication, individually and as a team. My leadership team and I were able to create a step change in mindset and profitability. I would strongly recommend that every team looking for a step change in measurable organizational deliverables read this book and take a close look at insight principles.

Alexander Wessels, CEO Archroma Management GmbH

A manifesto for the soul and the mind that is grounded in practical solutions which address our most pressing concerns and dilemmas. This is a thought-, ego-, and soul-provoking book. Even the most skeptical will come away feeling more in control and with deeper understanding of how thoughts and feelings work. Since reading the book I feel I am a better leader, a better mum, a better wife, and I'm better able to navigate emotionally ambiguous decision making.

This book is one of the top ten business books in my library and number one in its category. It's insightful, universal, authentic, practical, and funny.

You've got to read it!

Ilham Kadri, PhD, President, Diversey Care, Vice President and Officer Sealed Air

Coming from the field of design in a high-tech company, the understanding of insight principles has helped me both navigate the halls of corporate decision-making and allowed me to insightfully serve my customer in this rapidly changing technology world. On a personal level, I have seen growth in my clarity, sense of purpose, and skills as a leader. My team of highly creative and talented individuals, who were already performing at the top of their game, have also benefitted from this understanding, taking their contribution to an even higher level. This book is a must for teams who want to excel.

Curt Croley, Senior Director of Innovation and Design
Zebra Technologies (Formerly Motorola Solutions)

Feel like a victim of the hi-tech, 24/7 world of demands and expectations from others? Feel like your head is about to burst from all the things that you have to do? The good news is that you can have a highly productive and rewarding professional and personal life, if you understand some very simple things about how your mind works. Insight principles are very simple, and once understood, transform your ability to solve complex problems quickly and be more connected to the people who make up your life. This book is a must-read if you want to bring high performance and sustainability to your life.

Nick Gray, Strategic Projects and former VP of Human Resources Dow AgroSciences

This excellent book is a wonderfully simple and powerful introduction to the principles. Each chapter builds on its predecessor to give the reader an ever-deeper appreciation of the "invisible power" that is innate to us all. In using everyday examples from their own lives, the ordinariness of the authors and the universal nature of these principles shine through. As the authors point out, there is nothing for you to do to benefit from these principles. They are always at work; the important thing is to look in this direction. It turns out that happiness and peace is our birthright. Highly recommended!

Phil Hughes, Energy Industry Executive

This book is not just another business "how-to" book. It is both practical and far reaching in scope. It gets to the heart of the filter through which we all experience life—from the inside out—and calls into question the notion that there can ever be an "objective truth" to the human experience. I highly recommend this book for anyone looking to evolve their philosophy and gain a deeper level of enjoyment and success in both their personal and professional lives.

Michelle Richter, Chief Operating Officer Alesia Re, Ltd.

From the World of Human Development

In *Invisible Power*, Ken Manning, Robin Charbit, and Sandra Krot offer a uniquely new and extremely potent way of understanding and tapping into the hidden forces which shape our points of view, communication, and decision making. If you want (or need) to improve your business results, sit back, open your mind, and prepare to be amazed by what you see!

Michael Neill, international best-selling author of *The Inside-Out Revolution*

I found *Invisible Power* very insightful. It's profound and practical, clearly laid out and easy to read. There is a depth to every chapter and the book highlights very well the incredible insights of Sydney Banks. A must-read!

Elsie Spittle, International Three Principles Teacher
Author of *Wisdom for Life, Our True Identity, and Beyond Imagination*

I love *Invisible Power*. Its simplicity and clarity had me popping with insights, and its down-to-earth accessibility means I'll be recommending it to all my clients.

Jamie Smart, author of the best-selling book
CLARITY: Clear Mind, Better Performance, Bigger Results

The logic in this book is 180 degrees from mainstream thinking. Yet, the logic is refreshingly clear and compelling. There is no doubt in my mind that readers who grasp this logic will see their personal and professional game go to a higher level.

George Pransky, PhD, Senior Partner Pransky and Associates
Author of *The Relationship Handbook*

This book describes a new understanding of the power and limitless potential of the human mind. It reveals the very essence of business success and the role each person can play in creating a workplace that is thriving. The book is presented in a clear, accessible, and heartfelt way. I wholeheartedly recommend this to anyone interested in greater job satisfaction and productivity, ease in relationships, and higher levels of personal well-being.

Dicken Bettinger, EdD, Business Consultant, Executive Coach,
Founder of 3 Principles Mentoring

Invisible Power brings the invisible principles of human experience to the visible level in a most profound, practical, and conversational style. There are thousands of business books that have helped people improve their businesses, their management, and their leadership. This book stands out as unique and with more depth, by pointing to the invisible force behind how everything works. By going "behind the curtain" of how our psychological world works, the authors have revealed the simple secret to success, happiness, productivity, and making a real difference in the world of work and beyond. I will highly recommend it to all my consulting clients.

Joseph Bailey, Licensed Psychologist and author of the best-selling *Slowing Down to the Speed of Life* with Richard Carlson, *The Serenity Principle*, and other works

INVISIBLE POWER

INSIGHT PRINCIPLES AT WORK

EVERYONE'S HIDDEN INNER CAPACITY

KEN MANNING

ROBIN CHARBIT

SANDRA KROT

Insight Principles, Inc. - Lexington, MA

Printed in the United States of America
First Printing, 2015

ISBN: 978-0-9965305-0-7   Paperback
ISBN: 978-0-9965305-1-4   Hardback
ISBN: 978-0-9965305-2-1   eBook

Library of Congress Control Number: 2015910814

Insight Principles, Inc.
642 Marrett Road.
Lexington, MA 02421
USA

www.insightprinciples.com
www.invisiblepower.biz

Cover design by Rebecca Saraceno
Interior design by Stefan Merour
Edited by Elese Coit

TABLE OF CONTENTS

Part IV: Interpersonal Implications

PREFACE

The human dimension is as complex as it is fascinating. Having spent the majority of my career in HR and talent management, I have seen and experienced many approaches to personal and team development. The understanding outlined in this book brings a new paradigm of thinking about the human dimension. It is simple in its foundation, but incredibly rich and deep in its practice. For me, it has been a game changer in understanding human behavior and the profound impact our thinking has on our personal relationships and approaches to business challenges. These principles resonated with me greatly in my work as a HR practitioner, and were equally as relevant and useful to me as an operational business leader. Business is, after all, human.

Professionally, I have witnessed many individuals and teams become enlightened through their learning of the principles, resulting in breakthrough business and individual performance. Personally, the principles have given me a whole new lens through which to view the world around me, and a deeper ability to tap into my inner wisdom and instinct. This has in turn liberated me to be a better businessperson. And more importantly, a more grounded and present person to those I deeply care about. I hope your journey of discovery brings you similar insights.

Deborah Borg, President, U.S. Region, Dow Chemical Company

Acknowledgements

All authors know there are many behind-the-scenes contributors to a successful book. Here are the people we would like to acknowledge, to whom we owe an enormous debt of gratitude.

Once again we want to thank our friend and mentor, the late Sydney Banks. We are at a loss for words to adequately express our gratitude to him. Understanding the principles he uncovered has had an immeasurable impact on our lives.

There are individuals and organizations, too numerous to mention here, that we would like to acknowledge. Today they are sharing this understanding all over the globe, not only in business, but also in classrooms, hospitals, correctional facilities, in community revitalization projects, and with the homeless. We are proud to call them colleagues and we thank them for their heart-filled work.

Many colleagues and friends took the time to read early drafts of our book and to share invaluable recommendations. We can't thank you enough: Joe Bailey, Dicken Bettinger, Cheryl Bond, Cathy Casey, Greg Collins, Rolf Evenson, Antonio Galindez, Mara Gleason, Nick Gray, Michael Gordon, Phil Hughes, Leslie Miller, Michael Neill, George Pransky, Linda Pransky, Michelle Richter, Rita Shuford, Kathy Slivka, Jamie Smart, Elsie Spittle, and Stan Veltman.

3

Keith Blevens and Valda Monroe have been supremely influential in keeping us oriented toward a paradigmatic understanding of the human mind. Their insights about the inside→out paradigm, along with their friendship, provided us with essential clarity and direction for our writing.

To enable the production completion of this book, many people helped keep us on track and shape our thoughts into something more readable. First of all, thanks to Nikki Platte Nieves, a valued member of the Insights Principles team. She read the earliest versions of the book and shared her wisdom and expertise when we needed them most. Elese Coit, our editor, our friend and colleague, made our writing substantially better. Mark Chimsky gave us additional editorial advice that significantly improved the final text. Rebecca Saraceno took our ideas and created the striking cover for this book, and Stefan Merour created the right feel for the layout that we thought the book needed.

We also wish to thank the thousands of clients we have worked with over the years who graciously allowed us into their lives and into their companies. It has been an honor and privilege to partner with them. Their curiosity, openness, and dedication to continuous improvement allowed us to deepen our understanding and refine our approach.

For all the times we came late to meals because we wanted to write "just one more piece"; for the interrupted vacations; and for the missed movies, soccer and baseball games, and dog walks, we want to thank our families for their love and support.

To Kailia and Zander, Ken's wife and son, Ken sends a big thank you for all your patience and grace during this whole process and for reminding him what he was writing about when his thinking got the best of him.

From Robin to his best friend and love of his life, Sabine, heartfelt thanks for always believing, caring, and loving, and for doing anything you could to help.

To her partner, Peter Remick, Sandy wishes to say thank you for the times you picked up the slack and all the times you coaxed her outside into the fresh air.

INTRODUCTION

We are writing this book to share some great news—the best news we have ever heard.

This news has done more for us, for our clients, and for their businesses than anything we have learned. This book is about an invisible power you are using all the time. It is also about the competitive advantage of understanding this power.

We have shared this understanding with thousands of people, both individually and in teams. The understanding has enabled them to create previously unimaginable results (doubling the business's EBIT, solving long-standing intractable problems, uncovering and avoiding fatal business flaws, etc.). Companies that understand and tap into the invisible power we point to in this book will know how to be successful and continually find the insights needed to sustain success in a world that is changing at an ever-accelerating rate.

If you want specific details of what has been accomplished, please read on. This book is full of real-life examples and stories. While the stories are true, some of the details have been changed to ensure the confidentiality of our clients.

About Us and the Inspiration for Our Work

The three of us have decades of experience sharing an amazingly practical understanding of the invisible power of the mind. We work with companies of all sizes and types in the US and around the globe and are no longer surprised by the results they are achieving.

We have a passion, along with thousands of colleagues around the world, to share what has been profoundly impactful for us. Our inspiration for sharing the understanding in this book stems from our personal journeys of discovery with the work of Sydney Banks and what he illuminated about human nature.

Syd was a Scotsman and welder working in a foundry in British Columbia, Canada when he had an enlightenment experience that uncovered a crucial missing link in our understanding of human nature. In simple, practical language, he described basic truths behind our psychological experience—why we do what we do and why and how we experience what we experience.

These truths have existed in human knowledge and have been pointed to many times over thousands of years. Syd's simplicity made it easier for us, and our colleagues, to see how the mind works and to articulate this understanding to people from all walks of life, allowing them more productive and enjoyable lives.

It is not surprising that the more clearly and deeply you see how something works, the more effectively you can use it. This is true of your mind as well.

Our discoveries have motivated us to devote our work lives to sharing this understanding with others. Syd warmly and gently guided us with unique clarity. We are very deeply indebted to him. Some of the vignettes included in the book are about us, and you can read more about us and about Sydney Banks at the end of the book.

Meet Ken:

I have had a lifelong passion and interest in all things spiritual and psychological and have had a calling to help people have good lives. I grew up studying many spiritual traditions and pursued advanced degrees in psychology, eventually practicing as a psychologist for twenty years. In the middle years of my practice, I came across Syd's work and the principles we share in this book. They had a profound effect on my work and personal life. They helped me realize a simple set of answers to how the mind works. Personally, this greatly relieved my stress and anxiety and had a powerful uplifting effect. Professionally, I was amazed to see the quantum jump in results my clients experienced learning these principles.

Realizing these principles illuminated two things I had not seen in my decades of psychological and spiritual studies: 1) that people are innately mentally healthy and 2) that they are experiencing life through the power of their own thinking while mistakenly believing the power of their lives is outside themselves. When I saw these two facts, I immediately stopped doing a lot of what I had been taught to do with clients. A lot of the traditional methods I learned were not helping people very quickly, if at all, and I saw that many of these practices were based on incorrect assumptions. Letting go of these practices and helping people realize how their minds work proved to be a much more direct and powerful way to help people get on track and stay there sustainably.

In parallel to my career in psychology, I also have a strong background in business, having worked in various businesses with roles as national sales manager, director of marketing, and member of advisory or leadership boards. I am thrilled to be able to link the two facets of my work life, bringing these principles to organizations.

9

Meet Robin:

By the time I came across the principles, I had been fortunate to work for more than twenty years for two great companies. My first job was with Exxon, where I ultimately led a business with more than a half billion dollars in revenue. My second was as the practice leader for the chemicals industry at a large consulting company.

I worked with really smart, competent people—coworkers and clients alike. Despite the amazing accomplishments I had witnessed, I also saw a lot of variability. By this, I mean I often saw these same brilliant people make really, really bad decisions and stupid mistakes, despite their experience and abilities. As I reflected, I noticed, so had I! Somewhere in people was a variable that seemed to throw a monkey wrench into the works. Sometimes it was a small monkey wrench, but sometimes … not. Other than a bad cold, excess alcohol, or lack of sleep, there seemed to be no solid, factual explanation for this phenomenon—until I learned these principles. I then saw that people didn't need better processes or approaches; they needed to use the existing ones well. The human factor was the critical variable.

When I realized the actual inner workings of the human dimension for myself, I understood why the variability occurred; I understood that when people see how something actually works, their abilities increase dramatically.

I tested this understanding with a few colleagues and clients and saw the results. Whether it was helping someone address a long-standing issue in next to no time or easily smoothing out a difficult interpersonal issue, this new understanding was the missing link that I had been looking for in management science.

I also understood where my own moments of effortless, brilliant performance came from and what got in the way.

That was enough for me to realize I had stumbled upon something remarkable.

Meet Sandy:

I always wanted to help people. But after two degrees in the social sciences, countless professional workshops, and five years out in the field as a licensed mental health counselor, things weren't going so well. As much as I wanted to help my clients, rarely did I see them actually change. Teaching them how to better cope with their difficult circumstances was the best I could do. I knew I was missing something, so I kept attending classes and workshops.

In 1981, along with about a hundred other healthcare professionals, I attended a lecture given by the late Sydney Banks. I don't remember much about that lecture except one thing. He said we all live in a "world of thought." It took a while for the significance of those words to sink in. I had no idea that there was an invisible power shaping my and my clients' experience at every moment. I had no idea that this power held all the wisdom I would ever need to help my clients and to help myself. Gradually I had insights that would change both my personal and professional life. I finally found what I was missing.

Since then, my life's work has been to share an understanding of the invisible power of the mind with the world. For the first twenty years of my practice I specialized in working with individuals, couples, and families. I also headed a nonprofit counseling center. In 2000, I discovered the remarkable relevance this understanding held for business teams and business leaders, and they have been the focus of my work ever since. This book is a culmination of thirty-five years of research, experience, and insights that I feel fortunate to share with you. My hope is that your life will be touched as deeply as mine has been.

Invisible Power

The invisible power this book will point you toward resides in fundamental forces operating within your mind. We call these forces *insight principles*.

We like to think of insight principles as the interface between a simple spiritual truth and a pragmatic understanding of the mind. It is spiritual in the sense that it points to a living intelligent life force within you that operates beyond your personal control. It is pragmatic in that it deals with simple and observable principles that affect everyone all the time. These are constant and universal.

These principles are some of the most powerful forces in life, and always will be. They determine the shape, quality, and texture of your life. The purpose of this book is to point you toward seeing them for yourself. There is great power and benefit in realizing them.

This book will share the underlying understanding behind what we—and our clients—learned on our journey with insight principles. We will also show how realizing these facts for yourself not only puts you on a path toward more insight, but significantly increases the quality of your inner life, resulting in more balance, ease, and grace.

Can you imagine what your business would be like if breakthroughs were commonplace?

Can you imagine not being rattled by life's challenges, with the confidence that you can access new perspectives and solutions as needed for whatever comes your way?

Can you imagine a life with less stress and more joy?

This is what is on offer for you if you see what we are pointing to.

A Personal Note to you, the Reader

If you are like most of the people we work with, we know how busy you are. There is so much in your inbox to read that when you do get time to read, you likely have to skim much of it. We have a suggestion: rather than rushing through this book, read it in short doses. Read a few chapters at a time and then put the book down.

The power of this book is not in the words written on these pages, but in the insights generated within your mind. At a conceptual level, you may find the principles and their implications to be logical and/or philosophically interesting. Don't stop there. The power of your engagement with what you read comes when you allow insight to arise from within you and affect how you think, see, and feel. After many years, we find our realizations continue to deepen and enhance our psychological freedom, professional productivity, and joy in life.

Throughout the book, you will find highlighted callouts and reflection points. We put these in the book to help you slow down and allow for the digestion of what you are reading. We want you to receive as much nutrition from this book as possible.

As you read this book, we ask you to remember that the descriptions, concepts, models, and stories that we use are nothing more than pointers. It is easy, even tempting, to view these pointers as the thing we are trying to describe. It would be akin to reading a guidebook about Paris and thinking that it was Paris. Orientations are very useful, but to really see Paris, you have to go there.

If you take your time to realize, for yourself, what we are pointing to, we are confident you will come to know more intimately the innate wisdom, health, and capacity for insight designed into your core.

> **Any company's greatest untapped resource is the innate wisdom, health, and capacity for insight in its people.**

This is true for you as well.

Realizing what we point to in this book is a never-ending process. We are on our own journeys, and we hope this book contributes to your journey toward a fulfilling, productive life.

Bon voyage!

PART ONE

The Core

o n e

THE MISSING LINK

*Within the soul of all human beings, there lies an
innate spiritual knowledge that has the power to repair
mental disturbances ... not through analyzing their thoughts,
but by seeing the power of thought itself.*

~ Sydney Banks

There is a missing link in humanity's understanding of the way
the mind works. As we now see it, ignorance of this missing link
is responsible for much of the inefficiency and ineffectiveness in
business, as well as a great deal of unnecessary personal unhappiness
and suffering.

Most books on the human dimension in business focus on different
factors to help you be successful. Some look at your unique personality type, cultural background, or thinking style. They try to help
you understand your personality or suggest how to best interact with
others of different personality types. Others focus on relationships,
leadership, and performance. They suggest what you could or should

17

think or do to get better results. They provide attitudes, habits, and strategies to practice or adopt so that you can be successful.

Our book is oriented in a different direction. It focuses on the basic operating principles working behind the scenes of your human mind. When we refer to principles, we are not referring to ideas, values, or practices that you deliberately apply to your life. We are referring to facts of nature. We are pointing at the raw mechanics of experience, the invisible dynamics that operate within all people behind the scenes. These invisible principles are the missing link to understanding how to be at your best for whatever you do in life.

We will not prescribe things to think, do, or practice. There are no prescriptions or steps to apply. The intention of this book is to explain what we have shared with our clients so that you may also realize and see more of this invisible power.

A Platform of Understanding

Sydney Banks realized how our experience of life is actually shaped internally through a creative, invisible process. He articulated three basic truths, or fundamental operating principles, about the human mind which generate a new platform of understanding about how the mind works. These principles have far-reaching implications for how we know ourselves and each other and our effectiveness in business or any endeavor.

The Principle of Thought. The inherent, invisible, and ongoing power which crafts formless mental energy into your unique perceptions and moment-to-moment experience of life.

The Principle of Consciousness. The function (force) that illuminates and brings to life whatever you are thinking, allowing you to be aware and generating a sense of realness within your mind.

The Principle of Mind. The universal intelligence that exists in all things and makes life possible. Mind is not the brain. It is not a thing. It is, in essence, the life force creating the reality you see in every moment, whether you are conscious of it or not.

Syd helped us see that our internal creative process is more powerful than we will ever fully realize and that ignorance of how perception and feelings occur within us is the source of a great deal of difficulty in life. Embedded in our invisible creative process is a universal wisdom designed to guide us through life with a flow of useful insights. This wisdom orients us toward a balanced perspective and affords us the potential for rich, satisfying feelings.

In this book and in our work with businesses, we refer to these basic truths as insight principles. With insight principles as a foundation, we have found a way to point people to a depth of wisdom and insight that is incredibly useful in the world of business and a source of clarity and joy in life.

The power of this new platform of understanding rests on the fact that these three principles explain a dimension of human functioning operating behind the scenes of what you experience in your awareness. Because the principles operate before any specific thought or experience you may have, they hold the power of infinite possibility. Realizing the nature of these principles moment to moment affords you a great deal of psychological freedom.

The principles are the gifts that enable you to experience life. They are invisible and therefore easy to miss. You see the aftereffects and not the creative process they embody.

When you begin to wake up a bit to what is going on inside your mind, you have some leverage. You stop looking at external causes to blame for feelings or experiences you don't want to have. The next thing that can happen is that your attention goes to what you are thinking; in other words, your attention goes to the content of your thinking because this has now become more visible to you. If the content is troublesome, or if it is bringing you feelings you do not want, you naturally want to change this content. You might try to shift focus or think something more positive. Sometimes this works; often it doesn't.

There is a fork in the road.

Down one branch of the fork is a life of trying to fix the thinking you already have, chasing after what your thinking has manifested.

Down the other branch is a life of you seeing for yourself, in the moment, that the power lies in that invisible, formless place where your thinking comes from—and your potential lies—before you actually think anything. We are pointing to this branch.

The power is in the artist, not in what he paints. The power is in the thinker, not in what she thinks. This built-in capacity is the undervalued, often-ignored secret to your success.

Realizing Truth

There is great power in realizing what is true. The truth frees you from misunderstanding. The truth that Syd Banks articulated operates invisibly within the mind, just as gravity and magnetism work invisibly on physical matter. The principles he described shape and determine what you feel and perceive each moment, just as gravity determines what you weigh and how fast things fall when you drop them. The discovery of the previously invisible cell life of bacteria and viruses changed our understanding of disease and health care. So too, a realization of insight principles can be transformative—professionally and personally.

Understanding the facts of these living dynamics does three things:

1. It cuts through a lot of theories and guesses about what is going on with you and others.
2. It frees you from confusion about the source of your experiences and where your power and creativity in life truly lies.
3. It gets to the heart of what it takes to be at your best.

Realizing insight principles can be one of the most useful and powerful experiences you will ever have.

It has been for the three of us.

Principles Generate Implications

When you see the truth and logic of how something works, you can automatically apply that logic in a myriad of ways. Understanding the implication of these truths is far more powerful than adopting a set of practices, values, ideas, or attitudes.

One of the most powerful implications of Syd's discovery upends a current (but false) paradigm. You may innocently believe that external circumstances, situations, and/or other people determine your experiences, your feelings, and the quality of your life—that most, if not all, of what you feel and experience **happens to you**.

When you see these principles for yourself, you realize that your perceptions and feelings are generated within your own mind every moment. In other words, you experience life from the inside→out, even though it most often looks the opposite.

A second powerful implication of these principles is that you have a built-in design for success. The innate intelligence within is not only designed to help you survive but to thrive, whenever you are not getting in the way.

Though these two points may be intuitive to many of you reading this book, you may not realize that they are **always true**—no exceptions. We elaborate on this in the next four chapters.

Once you realize that your inner life is created in thought and that it can be transformed at any moment when your thinking changes, you see profound implications. In *Part Two—Basic Implications* and *Part Three—Personal Implications*, we look at the implications for some of the deepest aspects of your life: your personal identity, inner lifestyle, ability to connect with others, resilience, and how you understand and experience stress and time.

As this new platform of understanding plays out within you, it is only logical that you begin to see the far-reaching implications for your relationships, communication with others, and leadership ability. The last part of the book, *Part Four—Interpersonal Implications,* covers many of these topics.

The Untapped Potential: The Story of Mark's Team

To give you a sense of the potential we are pointing to, here's a real example of how learning about insight principles helped a business team transform their results.

We were asked to help a high-tech equipment manufacturer that had just been acquired by a leading global firm and was slated to become its crown jewel. The manufacturer's products were complex, sophisticated, and high quality, and the company was known for taking the market by storm, often reshaping the segment.

Here was the problem: it took twenty-one months to transition an idea to full commercialization. Prior to that, it took even longer—well over twenty-four months—but a team of sixteen professionals, highly trained in Six-Sigma™ and Lean™ methodologies and working over several years, had progressively cut down this time. The team had managed to shave off one month, on average, for every year of effort, and were aiming to cut another month off the transition time in the coming year.

Mark, the leader of this team, told us why this was taking them so long. "Shortening lead time was hard to figure out," he said. "If improving it were easy, others would have done it, and we are the industry leader."

Mark led a great team. They were smart, dedicated people committed to continuous improvement, always on the lookout for new ideas. They heard about our work and liked our logic. It was decided that half the team would work with us.

This group of 8 people, working part-time over fifteen business days, uncovered remarkably valuable insights that resulted in reducing the twenty-one-month lead time to eleven months! The decrease of almost 50 percent would create a one-off increase in earnings of $100 million. Mark was amazed and thrilled.

So how did eight people produce a result an order of magnitude greater than the prior efforts that had taken sixteen very intelligent people *years* of work? This was not low-hanging fruit. Filling in the missing piece of understanding about how the mind works made all the difference.

A Deeper Sense of Knowing

There are times when you experience a kind of knowing that feels deeper than your ordinary moments. You might call it a gut feeling, an intuition, or a quiet knowing. Some describe it as a feeling in their bones or knowing something from their soul. Heartfelt is another word.

Whatever you call it, you have this natural ability to know something deeply. Look for this deep sense of knowing as you read. It is your sign that you are realizing, for yourself, something powerful.

This deeper sense of knowing is your guide to the depth of what is on offer for you here. As you read, you will be reminded of the rich gifts within you that have guided you throughout your whole life, even though you may not have understood them.

As we mentioned in the introduction, take your time reading this book.

Let what you read soak in and touch a deeper sense of knowing in you.

In the next four chapters we lay the foundation that explains the extraordinary results our clients are witnessing.

In Summary:

- This book is descriptive and will not give you techniques or strategies to practice.

- Insight principles explain a true paradigm of how your experience of life is invisibly created from the inside→out.

- A deeper sense of knowing will guide your learning and accelerate the benefit of learning insight principles.

THE HUMAN MIND—
THE SHORT VERSION

*When you start to see the power of Thought and its
relationship to your way of observing life, you will better
understand yourself and the world in which you live.*

~ Sydney Banks

Here are the three important points we hope you understand after reading this book:

- Your mind works only one way.

- Your mind has a built-in design for success.

- Your life will be more productive, enjoyable, and fulfilling, the more deeply you realize the living truth of the first two points.

Your Mind Works Only One Way

There are certain things about life, about us, and about our world that fall into the following category: things that are true whether we know them directly or not.

As an example, humanity was once convinced that the earth was flat. We also unwittingly believed our planet to be the center of the universe. Of course, as we know now, the earth is round, revolves around the sun, and is just one speck of matter in a mind-bogglingly huge cosmos. These facts were true even before we fully understood them.

Gravity is another example of something that is true whether you realize it or not. We didn't always understand gravity and we rarely think about it in our day-to-day lives, but it is always there, operating behind the scenes, causing things to fall and keeping our feet on the ground.

Gravity is an invisible and powerful fact in your life. It is one example of how a force can have immense influence and yet you cannot see it. The invisible forces operating within your mind are perhaps even more powerful than gravity.

There are important truths about the human mind that exist and function within you—whether or not you know them consciously. These truths are present with you right now. These truths about the way your mind works are like the examples we just mentioned. They are true and already operating behind the scenes. Realizing their presence in your life will change your understanding of the world.

Your mind is the generator of your experience. Drawing on an unlimited source of creative energy, your thinking gets crafted from within, bringing you everything you see, sense, and feel in every moment. In other words, your moment-to-moment experience of life happens within you. It is created from the inside→out. Your mind always has, and always will, work this way.

The dynamics we are describing are the basic mechanics behind perception. We are referring to the fact *that you think*. We are not commenting on what you might think or experience at any moment; we are simply describing the way it works.

Your perceptions and feelings do not happen to you; they are created within you. They are your thoughts in action, brought to life in your consciousness. It is impossible to experience something without your thinking being involved. You won't see a beautiful sunset if your mind is not focused on it. You won't hear a subtle sound like the wind outdoors, the refrigerator humming, or the fan in the ventilation system unless your thoughts are directing your senses toward them. Without thought, a particular sense, impression, feeling, image, or idea cannot be part of your experience.

You are, no doubt, aware of yourself as a thinker to some degree and know that you use your thinking to manage your life every day. We are pointing to a subtle, deeper, and invisible level at which the power of thought operates. It happens so fast that you may never realize it. The principle of Thought shapes your inner life and what you experience in your senses. Because it is so unnoticed, you can easily mistake the source of your experiences and feelings to be other people or external circumstances.

It's easy to assume that your thinking is not involved in your perceptions, and you can fall into another common, but even more insidious, trap. You create realities in your mind and think they exist in the world, not recognizing that they are just your thoughts. Here is an example:

> You start thinking you need a bigger house or a nicer car
> to be happy or more comfortable in your life. You create an

image in your mind of what you want. Before you know it, you think the house you live in or the car you drive is **making you** unhappy. You don't realize you have created an alternate reality in your mind that you are now comparing your circumstance to. When imagining your desire, you feel anticipation or some sense that the future will have more joy in it. Your current situation seems lacking and feels bad, but, innocently, you fail to notice that you created all this in your own mind.

When we say your mind works only one way, or that you experience life from the inside→out, we are pointing to the basic fact that your thinking is the sole source of your experiences. We are also pointing to the fact that it is not logical that anything outside your mind can make you experience something without your own thinking being involved.

When you don't realize the primacy of thought at the core of your life, you fall into the notion that the outside world drives your personal life. This is a common myth that has been perpetuated for centuries in the absence of a clearer understanding. You can find this myth in nearly every book and newspaper you read. You can see it in movies and TV shows, and you hear it in song lyrics. It is a powerful myth we take for granted. It is at the root of business inefficiency and personal suffering.

We hope this book helps dispel this myth.

Your Mind Has a Built-In Design for Success

The second point we want to illuminate is as revolutionary, and as true, as the first. You have an innate set of inner psychological resources and processes that operates elegantly behind the scenes. These resources work effortlessly to keep your mind running, enabling you to understand life and live successfully with others in an ever-changing physical world. This built-in design for success affords you clarity, perspective, and insight when your mind is balanced.

To say this another way, there is an innate intelligence operating behind the scenes in your mind that is involved in everything you do, whether you are aware of it or not.

If you look closely, you will easily see that there is an intelligence running your body. This intelligence may not be visible, but it is observable in action. This intelligence is the life force that creates your bodily systems, beats your heart, heals the cut on your finger, and runs a host of other essential ongoing activities. You are not in charge of this force, but you benefit from it.

The same intelligence runs the mind.

Your mind, although elegantly designed and inclined toward your success, can produce undesirable outcomes when you misunderstand or forget how it is designed to work. The result can be much suffering and negative consequences.

The immune system is an excellent analogy. Prior to Louis Pasteur, bacteria were not known to exist. The common belief at the time was that people became ill due to evil spirits and foul air. Therefore, medical care did not pay attention to germs or hygiene and innocently tried to dispel those evil spirits or expunge the foul air in ways that hurt the body and compromised the immune system. Because people did not understand the design of the immune system, they failed to benefit from its natural design to keep us healthy.

With a fundamental misunderstanding about how the mind works, you may fail to live in harmony with your natural design, innocently overlooking the deeper gifts within you. What are these deeper gifts?

Simply put, you are designed for wisdom, insight, and joy. Your mind is designed to be in balance and to guide you intelligently through life.

The Invisible Power of Understanding Insight Principles

There are actually two invisible powers we refer to in this book.

The first is the invisible power of insight principles working behind the scenes, always generating your reality from within and affording you wisdom and insight.

The second invisible power is the transformative nature of **realizing** the truth of these facts in yourself. This realization can do more to improve your personal and professional life than anything we have come across.

The more you understand how something works, the better you adapt and make use of it. Whether it is your computer, a power tool, or your immune system, understanding enables you to take full advantage of the system.

When you understand the basic principles in any aspect of life, it changes how you know your world and what you can do within it. Discovering the principles of physics and aeronautics enables the 800,000-pound Boeing 747 to get off the ground. Understanding the principles of cell biology has led to the eradication of smallpox and the development of life-sustaining treatments for AIDS and many cancers.

With regard to your individual experience of life, realizing the principles of how your mind works will significantly change your life in a number of ways.

First, if you realize that your perceptions and feelings are generated in your mind, you stop seeing events, people, and circumstances as responsible for your inner experiences. You realize that the power to be internally balanced and find your own wisdom and common sense is inside you. Stress and upset can significantly diminish in your life, and may even disappear. You can have a life with more balance and psychological freedom. Your understanding functions like a self-correcting mechanism, allowing your mind to move to balance, clarity and well-being.

Second, you begin to see the invisible, immediate essence of your creative process alive in the moment. You live much more in the present and the quality of your presence becomes deeper and stronger. This happens as thoughts that are riveted on the past or worries about the future no longer seem as compelling. It is akin to turning a light on in a dark room cluttered with boxes and furniture. With light, you can easily get around without tripping over things, hurting yourself, or damaging the furniture.

Third, with more clarity and creativity, your life appears less fixed and riper with possibility. You come to know that your experience will change when your thinking changes, and you have a sense of a flow in life. You develop more faith that a fresh perspective is right around the corner. You find that you do not have to grind hard mentally to be clear and creative.

Lastly, and perhaps the greatest benefit of all, is that you can have a life with richer and more enjoyable feelings. You can learn to allow your system to naturally balance itself more easily and orient to what is positive and wise.

We are personally amazed at how much more energy, creativity, warmth, and love we have in our lives than we did before we learned insight principles.

One beautiful thing about realizing insight principles is that these benefits do not require practice or techniques. These shifts happen when you see the truth of how your mind works.

Realizing these principles was a life changer for Ken.

I learned about these principles just after I finished eleven years of formal education in psychology, including a PhD. I was a licensed psychologist in Massachusetts with a full psychotherapy practice, working assiduously to help my clients resolve their issues and stresses, using all that I had learned in graduate school. At my first principles program, I spent considerable time trying to convince my instructors that psychological change was more complicated than they were describing.

I left the training impressed with the instructors. They were gracious, patient, and not at all argumentative in the face of my wrangling about what they were teaching. I left thinking that it was a nice experience, but I didn't learn much.

In the car on the way to the airport, it hit me—psychological life is a lot simpler than I ever thought! I thought one needed to analyze and understand where things went wrong to become a clear-minded, healthy person. Instead, I realized that people don't see the power of thought to begin with, and that underneath all their thinking, everyone is fine and has a core of psychological health. We all have the gift of thought and the capacity for wisdom and insight. If everyone could see the essential nature of thought and the power it has, they would get out of their own way.

With his realization, Ken went back to his practice and began getting a new class of results in less time than he ever thought possible.

Realizing insight principles has great impact on relationships and teamwork as well.

When you realize the inside→out nature of perception, you see that everyone lives in a separate reality created by his or her own thoughts. You also understand that there is the same innate wisdom and potential for balance and well-being in everyone as there is in you.

As a result, you become more curious about other people's thoughts, realities, and whatever wisdom might be lurking behind what they are saying or doing. This often leads to deeper listening and understanding, which then leads to greater rapport and a sense of connection, which in turn leads to trust. With trust, alignment is easier and synergy tends to naturally occur as people work together on difficult problems with curiosity and openness.

For many of our clients in companies around the world, learning how the mind works has been a game changer.

This was the case for the high-tech company we mentioned in Chapter 1. Here is more of their story, highlighting the invisible power of understanding insight principles and the implications that follow from the understanding.

"This was a tough problem," explained Mark. "In fact, it was so tough, some called it impossible. And we had lots of historical proof! As the team learned about insight principles, it dawned on us that how a situation looked to us, whether it looked difficult or easy, was a function of the thinking we were entertaining. We could continue to think about the challenge the way we always had—and it would not change—or we could have an insight and maybe something would be different. We became increasingly curious."

"So why does it take twenty-one months?" asked Frank, the senior finance representative to this team.

"Well, the product is highly complex," said George, the VP of R&D. George was very proud of his team, which had developed the last few versions of technology that enabled their products to be manufactured.

"So what? Car manufacturers manage to redesign a car in twelve months, and that's pretty complicated," piped up Mary Lou, Mark's marketing VP, whom he'd chosen for this project because of her willingness to challenge traditional thinking.

"Well OK," came the reply from George, "but our production line has to produce three hundred million items per year with incredible accuracy, or people could be injured by our products."

"But still, they produce one million cars, and that's not simple either," said Mary Lou.

And so the discussion went on. Mark described it this way: "It wasn't a debate. It was more of a group reflection on what we didn't know. You could see people relaxing into the conversation. Even George, who rarely gets off his positions on things, started to have some fun, and was entertaining other people's ideas."

"This wasn't a technique or a process," Mark went on to say. "From a place of inner balance, we all naturally seemed to be wondering. Insights popped right and left. Some large, some frighteningly obvious!"

"By the end of the first meeting, we were mostly perplexed. Some great questions had surfaced, and a few answers had been found, too. We began to have faith that something would emerge from our collective wisdom. We knew that if we stayed in balance, we would eventually see something new and have the insights we needed. It was highly unusual for us to go to lunch without a solution and without stressing about it."

That afternoon, the dialogue eventually led to the topic of the production line. Although the company's products were less complicated than a car, the main cause of the long development process was the production line. Of the twenty-one months, about eighteen were consumed by the design and construction of the manufacturing equipment. Again, it had always taken a long time; after all, it was a very, very sophisticated piece of equipment. As they challenged the eighteen months, Mary Lou had an insight and asked the innocent question:

"What if we could get the line six months earlier? What would that save?"

Rather than object or condemn the question as ridiculous, the group reflected. "We did not worry whether it was doable, we just wondered," remembered Mark. A few quick calculations later, and the team had a figure of $40 million of profit.

"How much does the current line cost?" was the next question.

"About $20 million," said Frank.

"So why don't we pay the line supplier an extra $10 million and get the line quicker?" said Mary Lou.

All hell broke loose for a moment. "This was impossible!" "It couldn't be done!" was the predominant thinking in the room.

"You can probably imagine the reactions many in the room were having," Mark told us. "But we quickly settled. We kept catching ourselves getting caught up in reactions, and then we'd calm down and reflect on what was being said."

As the team kept dialoguing, it came out that one of our repeated strategies to improve profitability had been to beat down the price that we paid the line supplier. The lines had cost almost $30 million in the past, but through years of effort we had been able to reduce its cost by almost 30 percent. No one had really thought about lead times, which remained mostly the same. We were now really curious … if we spend $10 million more, we can make an additional $40 million! Although a few people still wanted to question, the logic was starting to look compelling."

Frank finally concluded that, from a finance point of view, this was brilliant, and there was no reason not to fully explore the possibility.

Within the next six weeks, the team and the line manufacturer agreed on the deal. The manufacturer was glad to have the revenue, and Mark's team was able to get their products to the market almost ten months sooner than they thought possible.

The story of Mark and his team portrays the powerful shift that comes with a clear understanding of how the mind truly works. Egos softened and trust developed quickly as stress and reactivity melted away. Rapport deepened, and everyone felt more connected and lighthearted in the face of a big challenge. The synergy that arose as the collective wisdom in the team flowed produced a remarkable result in record time.

The next three chapters of the book will illuminate, in more detail, the three main points we outlined in this chapter. In the later parts, we will show how these points create a platform of understanding with a potent set of implications for living, relationships, and team functioning—in and out of the workplace.

In Summary:

- Your mind works only one way.
- Your mind has a built-in design for success.
- Your life will be more enjoyable, productive, and fulfilling the more deeply you realize the living truth of these two points.

three

YOUR MIND WORKS ONLY ONE WAY

Someone once said to me, "Are you telling me
that chair isn't real, that it's only a thought?" I said,
"Of course the chair is real, but it comes to you via thought."

~ Sydney Banks

The sun rises every morning.

Or does it? It certainly looks that way. We know that the sun is relatively stationary in our sky and it is the earth that is turning on its axis, causing the sun to appear to change its position in the sky. This fact is "invisible," but if you think about it, you can see the truth of it.

On any given day, if we asked you why you feel the way you do, you would likely point to a source outside yourself. You might say the traffic, the weather, or your spouse caused your feelings. You might even blame all three! And yet, at times, you would also know that your thinking alone was the culprit.

41

We humans comfortably, and unconsciously, alternate between two different paradigms explaining where our experience is coming from.

The outside→in paradigm holds that your feelings and experiences are caused by events in the external world. Somebody or something makes you feel the way you do. Your thinking is a logical reaction that follows circumstances and events. For example, one of your kids misbehaves and you think he or she is causing you to be angry. It doesn't look like the anger has anything to do with your thinking.

The inside→out paradigm holds that your thinking creates your experience of reality. No situation, person, or event can make you feel a certain way or make you have a certain experience. You will feel and experience whatever you are thinking in the moment. For example, one of your kids misbehaves and you get angry. You know that the kid's behavior cannot make you angry, only your thinking can do that—which is why sometimes you don't get angry when they misbehave.

These paradigms are mutually exclusive. The inside→out paradigm is the only one that is true. The outside→in paradigm is a misunderstanding similar to the misunderstanding, about the sun and the earth.

Whether you realize it or not, ALL of your experiences, feeling states, and realities derive from a creative process happening inside your own mind.

Here's an amusing story that happened to Sandy many years ago:

When I was much younger, I was invited to attend the opera by my boyfriend. I had never been to the opera before, so this opportunity was thrilling. I bought a new dress, had my hair and nails done, and arrived at the opera with my boyfriend in a state of anticipation and joy.

We had planned to meet another couple in the lobby, and finally we spotted them in the crowd. My boyfriend greeted Mary Catherine, the woman in the couple we were meeting, with these exact words: "Mary Catherine, you look so lovely! You are the most beautiful woman in the room!" I was standing right next to Mary Catherine at that moment.

Mary Catherine looked over at me with an extremely uncomfortable look on her face and blurted out, "Oh no! No! Doesn't Sandy look more beautiful?" Poor Mary Catherine, she felt so bad. I'm sure she was thinking that my feelings were hurt by what my boyfriend had just blurted out—that he thought another woman, not me, was the most beautiful woman in the room.

Believe it or not, I found it hilarious! In fact, I laughed so hard that the people nearby started staring at me. To this day, I cannot tell the story without laughing. I never once felt hurt or insulted by my boyfriend's comments. For whatever reason, his words struck me as funny. Inside my mind at that moment (and for the rest of the evening, whenever I recalled the interaction), no hurtful thinking ever occurred to me. All I could think about was the hilarity of it all.

Sandy did not try to find her boyfriend's comments funny. She wasn't giving him the benefit of the doubt either. The thoughts that came to her in the opera lobby were funny thoughts, so she had a funny experience. If Sandy had bothered, insecure, or upset thoughts, she would have felt those feelings instead. This is the way the mind works.

A Built-In Movie Studio

You perceive everything in life in your mind. Every moment of the day, your mind is crafting and shaping your experience and feelings. External circumstances, people, and events are not the cause. The power of your creative process is absolute and within you. It has always been this way. It will always be this way.

We are not implying that you are responsible for other people and things in life, for the world, or for how life works.

We are saying that your mind is completely responsible for the way you experience life and what you feel. This is true not just in the way you react to things, but also in the way life looks to you in the first place. Inside your mind, using the principles of Thought and Consciousness, your thinking shapes, colors, and sets the tone and texture of everything you experience.

Picture a crowded, busy sidewalk in Manhattan, for example. Crowds of people pass each other and the city around them. People have their own thoughts, perceptions, and feelings. These thoughts, perceptions, and feelings constitute their experience, and this experience morphs and changes each second. Different things show up in their senses, if they notice their senses at all.

On his way to a meeting, a man smells a hot dog stand and suddenly realizes he's famished. The woman walking next to him doesn't notice the smell of hot dogs at all—her thoughts are focused on safely crossing the intersection. One person feels compassion for a homeless panhandler, another feels contempt, and a third person doesn't even notice. Same circumstance, and yet an infinite number of reactions are happening in each moment. And each personal experience seems utterly real and poignant.

Your own experiences are constantly shifting. You may have a lot on your mind or not much. You may have no sense of time and are able to enjoy the present, or you can be stressed and hurried and feel completely out of time. Sometimes you may be full of thoughts about yourself. Sometimes you may have no sense of self at all, just a love for life, intense focus on a task or project, or concern for someone else.

Your mind, like a movie production studio, continually creates a new scene with feeling and meaning.

The invisible power you use to think and create exists within. Without realizing this invisible power in your life, you most likely think that your senses function the way a camera does, taking in the world objectively.

But your senses do not work that way.

Your senses cannot discriminate what to pay attention to or what meaning to attach to things. Your senses are controlled and informed by the power of thought. Without that power, your five senses would not work. If you watch closely, you will see that at times your senses don't seem to be functioning at all. As you read this, you might find yourself remembering a conversation from yesterday and your attention will be fully absorbed experiencing that memory. Your mind recreates the sensory experience of yesterday and overrides anything happening in the moment.

Dreaming is an interesting case in point. When you are asleep and not connected to your outer senses, thoughts come into your mind, and your mind creates a sensory movie you experience as a living reality. You experience, feel, and react to it fully.

You do this while you are awake as you imagine or daydream realities that could be. You then come out of your reveries and realize you were dreaming or imagining.

What you don't fully recognize is that the process of thought is at the core of everything you experience all day long. Your daily life is your dream that changes moment to moment as your thinking changes. You only have to compare how wonderful everything seems on a good day and how challenging it can be when your mood is low. One day you are grateful for your family and job, and the next you are ready to trade one or both in for something else. The world has not changed that much, but your waking dream has.

You live in a world of thought.

Simple and Profound

The idea that your thinking creates your reality is likely not new to you, and we are certainly not the first people to point out this phenomenon.

You may have heard it said that:

- Perception is reality
- Attitude is everything

- We see what we want to see

- And so on …

When we say that your mind can only work one way, we are leaving no wiggle room, no exceptions, and no exclusions.

Ask yourself this question and take a moment to reflect on it.

What if it didn't work the way we describe? What if circumstances, other people, the past, etc., could somehow get into your mind and make you feel a certain way?

Let's look at a familiar travel event experienced from different paradigms. Each of the following scenarios describes how the event would look to you, how you might react, and the result, depending upon your understanding of how the mind works.

Scenario 1: *Thinking is not involved in my experience of reality.*

You have been assigned a middle seat on a completely full flight. As you board the plane, you notice two bodybuilder-sized guys seated in your row. You squeeze yourself into your seat and immediately feel uncomfortable.

You think, "Why me? How come I always get stuck in the middle seat? Why do the airlines make these seats so small? This is awful. I hate sitting in the middle. This is going to be a long, miserable flight."

As the plane takes off, you feel more and more cramped and uncomfortable. It doesn't look like your thinking has anything to do with your feelings. It looks like the middle seat is causing your discomfort. You continue to complain to yourself. You hoped to finish some work on the plane, but you can't focus. All you can think about is how miserable it is to be in the middle seat.

The flight drags on, and there is no relief until the plane lands and you get off. Even in the terminal, your mood remains irritated as you call your spouse to rant about what you just went through.

Without awareness of your inner creative process, you live as though you are seeing an objective reality through your senses and are responding or reacting appropriately, as if your thinking has nothing to do with what you experience. You believe you are a victim of circumstances.

Scenario 2: Thinking affects my perceptions and attitudes.

You have been assigned a middle seat on a completely full flight. As you board the plane you notice two bodybuilder-sized guys seated in your row. You squeeze yourself into your seat and immediately feel uncomfortable.

You begin to think, "Why me? How come I always get stuck in the middle seat? Why do the airlines make these seats so small? This is awful. I hate sitting in the middle. This is going to be a long, miserable flight."

Since you have some understanding that your thinking determines your attitudes, feelings and behaviors, it occurs to you that if you are not careful with your attitude, you will go down a slippery slope into a really bad mood. You decide to manage your thinking and be careful not to let your negative attitude ruin your flight. It doesn't occur to you that the situation is negative because of your thinking—it seems truly negative—but you need to control your reactions to it. You tell yourself to look on the bright side. At least you have a seat on the plane. You remind yourself you are headed home. You find something to be grateful for.

You feel cramped and uncomfortable, but you are able to refocus as you open your laptop to work. As long as your focus holds, the discomfort of the cramped quarters is bearable, and your grumpy thinking doesn't get any traction. You congratulate yourself on your ability to keep yourself relatively balanced.

The flight drags on. When the plane lands and you walk up the jetway, you notice a tightness in your shoulders, which makes you realize how tired you are. You call your spouse to describe how you were able to overcome a bad circumstance.

With this understanding, you see thinking as a factor in life. You see it as a process occurring after the fact of your experience. Your thinking looks like an interpretation of what comes in to you from your senses, not the essential creator of your perceptions and feelings.

As such, you still have to manage your thinking to keep it positive and productive. You have to check it, reframe it, let it go, analyze it, express it, find a new interpretation, stop it, or something else. You end up with a mental workload in addition to the life workload you already have.

Scenario 3: *Thinking is the sole source of my personal reality.*

You have been assigned a middle seat on a completely full flight. As you board the plane you notice two bodybuilder-sized guys seated in your row. You squeeze yourself into the seat and immediately feel uncomfortable.

You begin to think, "Why me? How come I always get stuck in the middle seat? Why do the airlines make these seats so small? This is awful. I hate sitting in the middle. This is going to be a long, miserable flight."

At some point while your discomfort is building, it eventually occurs to you to wonder, "Where is this feeling coming from?" It looks like it is coming from being in the middle seat between two big guys who can't help but impinge on your space—especially the armrests! But you remember that experiences don't work that way. You realize that your head is filling up with a bunch of thoughts generating annoyance and bother. You know that as long as you keep thinking what you are thinking, you are going to keep feeling what you are feeling. You see, once again, that this is just the way the mind works.

You begin to see your thoughts of annoyance for what they are: just thoughts. The annoying thoughts seem less compelling and begin to drop away. Your escalating discomfort eases, and you are grateful that your understanding and insight have headed off an episode of serious grumpiness. You are still on a crowded plane seated between two big, burly guys, but your mind turns to other matters. You get out your laptop and start to work.

Periodically you think about your surroundings. You have moments of discomfort. You might even entertain thoughts of bother and annoyance, but they don't look worthy of paying much attention to. Eventually the plane lands, and you call your spouse to say you have landed safely.

When you see for a fact that the mind can only work one way, you also know that situations never make you feel anything unless your thinking is involved.

You can never experience anything but your own thinking. It's just not possible. Seeing this fact is like releasing the emergency brake of a sluggishly moving car. In the next moment, performance improves.

It's not *what* you think that matters, but *that* you think.

Why Thought is So Hard to See

You have probably experienced each of the scenarios above, but our guess is that Scenario 1 is far more common. If your mind only works one way, why don't you see the role of thought in your life more often?

There are two reasons:

1. The creative process is invisible and fast.
2. Most of humanity lives with a misconception about how the mind really works.

Let's spend a moment on each of these.

1. *The creative process is invisible and fast.*

Your mind creates a compelling reality, but it does not look as if thought creates it. Without any disclaimer or warning, your thinking immediately creates a sensory experience within you that looks real to you. It will continue to look real until you think something else.

> **It is impossible to consistently catch yourself in the act of thinking. It is like magic: you see the illusion, but not how the magician created it.**

One of our clients works for a software company whose products are used in Apache attack helicopter simulators. A few years ago, his team was invited to their client's training center to experience the product that used their software. Here's how he described what happened:

The training center was a nondescript hangar housing several simulators. The simulators were basically big black boxes mounted on pistons. I climbed into one and strapped myself into an aluminum seat at the back. At that point I was in a well-lit, metal and plywood box, with walls covered by several LCD screens and many instruments and controls.

The lights were extinguished, the simulator powered up, and within seconds I found myself flying across the desert, at over 150 miles per hour. At fifty feet in the air, I swooped around the contours of the terrain, accompanied by a deafening *whop-whop-whop-whop*. As this went on,

> my heart rate accelerated and I was actually bracing myself for the 150 mph turns!
>
> I couldn't believe it! How could I forget I was in a simulator box and not an Apache helicopter?

So, how could he forget he was in a simulator that he created and believe he was really flying? You would think he'd be pretty hard to fool.

But this is the inside→out creative process at work! He wasn't tricked by his senses; he was tricked by his thinking! It rarely seems like the mind is the source of perception.

All this happens fast because of the invisible power of thought. You don't realize how powerfully thought creates the context in which you perceive things and determines your perspective. You don't realize how powerfully thought directs what to pay attention to and what to ignore.

2. Most of humanity lives with a misconception about how the mind really works.

As a species, we operate under the spell of an incorrect paradigm. We assume the mind works like a camera, objectively recording life as it is, and that only afterwards do we think about it and react to it.

The fundamental misunderstanding that outside circumstances cause your experience is reinforced everywhere.

Sporting events are a great example. Your favorite team wins the championship, and you feel happy. The whole town feels happy. There may even be a parade. On the local news, commentators tell of the town's joy because of the team's result. They don't say, "The team won and many people are having happy thoughts about it," they actually say the win is making everyone happy.

In many shops, businesses, offices, schools, and homes, people agree that the win made them happy. Yet, there are countless people who could not care less about sporting events. How come the team's win isn't making them happy?

We are not saying that any of these experiences are more or less valid or better than the others. We *are* saying that *all* experiences and feelings about the winning team are created through an individual's thoughts about the event.

Worry and anger are examples that most people can relate to regarding this point. To worriers, the world looks like a scary place where things go wrong. To the angry person, the anger looks like a justified response. We are not saying that people should or should not feel angry or worried. We simply want you to see the actual source that is generating those perceptions and feelings.

Until the three of us came across this understanding, we too believed that our senses simply took a snapshot of the way the world is. We agreed that perception is reality; nevertheless, we attributed our perceptions and our feelings to the outside world. We would say things like, "the traffic drove me crazy," "I was happy after I got the news," etc.

Just to be clear and honest, you will still hear these statements come out of our mouths periodically. We forget how the mind works all the time. But inevitably we remember, and that has made all the difference in our lives.

In Summary:

- Your mind can only work one way, from the inside→out.
- It's not what you think that matters, but that you think.
- Your experience will always look real.
- The power that creates your reality from within is invisible and faster than you can ever realize.

four

Your Mind Has a Built-in Design for Success

Everyone in this world shares the same innate source
of wisdom, but it is hidden by the tangle of our
own misguided personal thoughts.

~ Sydney Banks

Jim Abbott is an example of someone who achieved remarkable results in life. Even more remarkable is that he did so in the face of a disadvantage most of us will never face. Jim may or may not have been able to articulate how or why his mind had a built-in design for success, but he is a living example of it.

In 1993 Jim Abbott pitched a no-hitter for the New York Yankees. The list of people who have pitched a complete game in Major League Baseball without allowing one hit is very short. The list Abbott is on is even shorter, because Abbott was born without a right hand.

Early in his career, Abbott was interviewed by a television reporter who asked him a rather predictable question: "What is like to pitch with a handicap?" Abbott replied with a straight face, "What handicap?" Flustered, the reporter blurted, "You don't have a right hand!"

As if this was news to Abbott.

Abbott finally let the reporter off the hook and graciously explained that he'd never thought of himself as handicapped. His parents did not use the term handicapped and did not treat him differently from his siblings. He loved baseball and pitching, and it simply never crossed his mind that he couldn't compete.

Without thinking about limitations, Abbott's innate talent rose unfettered to the surface.

The beauty of Jim's story is that it illustrates how the innate capabilities of his mental equipment allowed him to achieve his success. It never occurred to him that he was limited. He did not conjure up positive thoughts. In the absence of any thinking about his condition, the system seemed to provide him everything he needed. Though Jim certainly had a great environment in which to create his success, we are interested in the inner resources that allowed him to stay on the cutting edge of his creative journey.

We are not intending to be inspirational here, just pragmatic about the fabulous equipment you have inside. If you understand these basic capacities within yourself, you will naturally see how to be at your best more easily. Your life and your results will also be much more enjoyable and rewarding.

The internal mechanics of life are miraculous and operate invisibly behind the scenes while you are busy doing things and thinking about what you are interested in. Learning about your innate mental capacities can save you a great deal of time and energy, as well as enable more productivity and joy.

Let us explain.

Suppose you realized that you have a source of insight and wisdom in you that can deliver perspective and creative thinking related to any problem you will ever encounter. Would you spend a lot of time tearing your hair out to solve every issue in your life? Or would you step back, reflect, and have faith that you will see what you need to see when you need it?

With awareness and understanding of your own mental resourcefulness, you can push less and get more done. You have more wisdom, insight, and creativity than you can imagine.

You can also have a nicer life in the process. You'll find that relationships become richer and more effective. You will find synergy with others more easily.

To help you see how the mind is designed for success, think of a time when you were at your best. How would you describe yourself during this time?

Here are some qualities we have heard:

- Clarity
- Focus
- Humor
- Perspective
- Compassion
- Joy
- Common sense

- Presence
- Know-how
- In a flow
- At ease

Have you ever had a very complex problem to solve and when you started, you noticed you were unusually relaxed and curious? Did a great idea about how to proceed come to you seemingly out of nowhere?

Have you ever found yourself fully absorbed in what another person was saying and surprised by how easy it was to grasp the point and hear more subtle messages behind the words? Was it a joy to get to know the person, and did you come away feeling a deeper sense of understanding and connection than you expected?

Have you been in a crisis situation and acted with swift precision, even though you had no prior experience in such a crisis? Instead of feeling afraid and frozen up, were you energized and clear and knew what needed to be done without thinking about it?

Did it feel like you were making yourself be your best? Were you working at being clear, focused, funny, engaged, etc.? Or did those qualities show up when you needed them, given what you were doing and in response to the situation you were in?

•————————————————————•

Take a moment and reflect on the many effortless, intelligent things you do in any given day without having to think about them.

•————————————————————•

This is the built-in design for success we are pointing to.

Your Innate Intelligence

Life is a miracle that we often don't pay much attention to. You are a small part of that miracle, just like a drop of water in an ocean is a part of a bigger whole.

Your body is designed to maintain itself and heal. Your heart pumps essential oxygen and nutrients to every organ. Your brain is a sophisticated computer that allows you to have a mental life, to learn, and to remember. Your immune system protects you from invaders. While you can influence these processes, you are not running the show. There is a living intelligence in the body doing it for you.

Your mind is part of that same living intelligence, providing you with the tools for a successful life.

- Your mind wakes you up each day, enabling an awareness of the world.
- You have the capacity to think purposefully about things. Whatever you are thinking will occupy your mind and fill up your experience until you think something else. Can you imagine the instability of life if this weren't the case?
- You have the ability to create an infinite array of scenarios and realities in your imagination. Can you imagine life without this creative ability? What if you were just an information-processing machine?
- You were born with the capacity for awareness and reflection so that you can know what is going on within your mind. Without this awareness, you would be a slave to whatever showed up in your mind at any minute.
- You can know something deeply and be touched by life.

- You can struggle with a problem, leave it alone, and then, out of nowhere, the solution pops into your head. Where did the solution come from? How is it that the mind comes up with such insights out of the blue?

The list goes on and on.

Your Human Operating System

Behind your thoughts and concerns is a fabulous operating system designed for your effectiveness and success in life. Just as a cell phone has an operating system enabling it to do all the neat things you like it to do, so does your mind. When it comes to your phone, you usually don't think of the hidden operating system unless something goes wrong. Chances are you rarely stop and reflect on the brilliance of how your mind functions behind the scenes.

When you have less thinking on your mind, your background operating system will bring you clarity and a flow of thoughts that will be responsive to your needs or situation. You can jump out of the way of a speeding car or do anything else you need to do. Have you ever noticed how naturally you move from one moment to the next without effort when you are relaxed, and how feeling centered and grounded can happen effortlessly?

We sometimes refer to the experience of being in flow, feeling centered and grounded, as "being at home in yourself," or being balanced. You feel like you can think for yourself; you have perspective and common sense. Being present, aware, grounded, and at home inside yourself are not things you "do." Your internal operating system does all this for you naturally from within.

You can experience balance in a crisis or difficult situation, just as in any other ordinary moment. With adrenaline pumping through your system and your body in high gear, your mind can be crystal clear and highly responsive with a flow of useful insight. A great example of this is an athlete at the top of his game. Athletes call this "the zone," and they know what to do next, almost without having to think about it.

Can you imagine if your basic operating system didn't work this way and didn't naturally bring you back to balance and presence of mind? You would have to be vigilant and control your mind constantly. You could never rest.

Here's our client, Phil's, story:

It was the evening of Day Two of my team's insight principles program. I had been really struck by what I had learned. I couldn't really describe it yet, but it felt true and profound. It was about 7:30 pm, dinner was over, and I was minding my own business, musing on the day, when my doorbell rang. I got up to see who was at the door, admittedly feeling a bit bothered by being disturbed during my quiet time. At least that's how I was thinking about it!

At the door was a woman with a clipboard. Without much introduction, she launched into a rabid speech about the political candidate she was supporting. Although she did not know it, I was a fervent supporter of the opposing candidate.

I noticed my blood was starting to boil, and it was familiar. Many a poor soul had been marched off my front porch. As my anger rose, I remembered what I had just learned: nothing outside of me could cause me to experience something without me thinking about it, and the strength of feeling in me was only an indication of the strength of the thinking I was entertaining.

I actually started to settle down, which was definitely not my m.o. Most often my feelings would take over and I would say things I'd later regret. This time it was easier to let it all go.

My attention then went back to the woman. She looked so tired, and even though she continued to rant on, oblivious to my lack of interest, I started to wonder what sort of day she had had. How many Phils had she run across?

From somewhere in me I felt all this compassion for the woman, and interrupted her midsentence: "Are you OK? You look really tired. Can I get you something?" She paused, her shoulders slumped, and she replied, "Actually, it's been a hard day. I'd really love a cup of coffee." I suggested she sit down on the chair on the porch, and I went inside to make her a cup, somewhat incredulous about what was happening—grumpy me was making coffee for an uninvited stranger who'd shown up to spoil my evening!

When I returned with the coffee, I sat in the other chair while she slowly drank. "This is just what I needed," she said, "no one has been listening to me all day." I resisted the urge to explain why and just sat there, feeling grateful that I had been able to help someone. Then she looked over and asked, "You're not all that interested in my message either, are you?" I replied honestly that I wasn't. A few minutes later she got up, thanked me, and left.

I had this deep feeling of gratitude. In the past, such a visitor would have been the start of an outburst of anger and frustration, and a ruined evening. What a difference.

Phil didn't decide to be a more gracious person or to conquer his habit of getting annoyed at interruptions. Both strategies had failed him countless times. He saw his thoughts creating annoyance clearly enough to avoid getting caught up in them. His common sense and compassion arose in place of them.

As soon as the campaigner's thinking cleared, her perspective and common sense returned, and she saw it was time to go home. One might attribute her shift to Phil's kindness and generosity, but if her thinking never cleared, she could have easily remained pushy or gotten annoyed herself.

When our mind is free, our innate design brings us back into balance and moves our system toward well-being.

> **You don't have to work hard to be well.**

You just have to get out of the way and allow your natural design to function as it is designed to. If you are one of the many who have forgotten (or never realized) that you are designed to have healthy and successful mental functioning, you probably feel stressed and don't rest very much. It doesn't have to be this way.

A Light in the Dark

Your mind also has the power to create enormous suffering and to drive you to act without wisdom, common sense, or humanity. If you fail to realize the inside→out nature of experience and that you are designed for health and well-being, you can live an unbalanced life with little happiness or humanity. A brief look at any newscast, newspaper, or human history is all you need to find ample examples of this. You probably have quite a few examples in your own life as well.

63

Understanding the invisible power of thought and the invisible working of your built-in design for success can be a light in the darkness in a world full of pain and confusion.

Those who mistakenly believe their feelings and experiences come from people, circumstances, and events outside themselves can innocently be taken for a ride wherever their thinking may lead them. Some folks go their whole lives innocently believing this is normal and subsequently live with the repercussions. Whenever we are lost in thought—without seeing it as thought—it will become our reality and guide our feelings and actions.

Our lives have changed considerably since we realized we have a built-in design for well-being and success. We are much quicker to see our reactions and troubled thoughts for what they are and spend less time feeling stressed, upset, or bothered. It looks logical and ordinary to live with good feelings and a balanced perspective, and less logical not to. As such, we have more access to our hearts and our wisdom and find our relationships with others are warmer and more fulfilling than ever. We also find we have more creative energy and insight to be productive.

The same is possible for you.

In Summary:

- An intelligence exists in all things that makes life possible. Your mind is part of this intelligence. When you forget this intelligence exists, you tend to overthink, overanalyze, and overwork.
- Your mind is designed to move you toward balance with insight and well-being at any time.
- Realizing the living miracle and capacity of your built-in design for success enables you to relax more and work with your inner resources instead of pushing yourself too hard.

five

THE INVISIBLE POWER OF UNDERSTANDING

With our intellect, we discover.
With an insight, we uncover.

~ Sydney Banks

Do you remember the movie *The Wizard of Oz*?

After the "Wizard" is discovered behind the curtain, Dorothy and the Good Witch of the North have a conversation.

The Good Witch reveals to Dorothy that she always had the power to go home within her ruby slippers. Dorothy is a bit miffed and asks why she wasn't told this. The Good Witch replies, ever so knowingly, "You wouldn't have believed me." Eventually Dorothy recognizes that the Good Witch was right: she had to see the truth for herself.

We are all like Dorothy, searching for answers along the "yellow brick road." As we go along, we are deluged with information, techniques, strategies, and rituals for a better life.

Like Dorothy, it is important to understand where to look. It is important for you to see for yourself that what you seek is already inside. All efforts to solve your life's problems with a misunderstanding of where your true power lives will never work.

There is a great power in realizing truth. A simple yet profound understanding of the nature of thought frees your mind to be balanced, with a flow of clarity and insight. This is so much faster and more effective than working hard to analyze and change your thinking.

The invisible power of this understanding is at the heart of everything we are pointing to in this book. This power has been guiding you throughout your entire life.

"Hey, I have a hand and I can use it to grab stuff."

"Look, I found my balance, and I'm standing."

"Wow, walking is awesome!"

"Those scratchings on the page are letters. I can read."

"That bicycle looks like fun. Hey, I'm riding on my own! Boy, it hurts when I fall off."

You get the picture.

A memorable example happened for Robin in his last year of university.

I was struggling through an unbearable and unfathomable class on process control—the mechanical, process-bound, and highly mathematical understanding of how complex manufacturing plants were automated. Essentially, it was like the inside of the thermostat in your living room, but at an industrial level.

The lecturer was a sweet guy, but a lousy lecturer.

To be able to do research at the university, he had to teach a class, and so he did, or rather tried to. In addition, my university had a "sudden death" approach to grading. If you failed even one of your final exams, you would fail the entire academic year. You can probably imagine my concern when, half a year into this class, I remained surrounded by the fog of confusion, unsure it was going to lift. Just for context, 75 percent of my classmates were in the same predicament.

Then I got lucky.

In one very memorable class (at least for me), I suddenly saw something I had not seen before. I had a moment of understanding—insight. The lecturer was droning on as usual. I wasn't especially tired or alert; I remember him saying something. I only remember that it was very simple, and I heard it differently than anything I'd heard him say before.

In that instant, the disparate collection of thoughts that, until that point, had constituted a very confusing course, suddenly fit together, made sense, and created a new whole—one that I could understand. I saw the invisible framework the professor was not articulating. Everything the lecturer had been saying for nearly five months fell into place. He was still an unskilled lecturer, but I (thank goodness!) clearly saw what he was trying to explain. I also remember turning to a classmate and pointing out what I had just heard and how helpful it had been, only to get a blank stare in return.

What had been invisible to Robin was now visible, but not yet to his classmate.

> **Understanding makes the invisible visible.**

Depth of Understanding

As a model to illustrate what we mean by depth of understanding, let's use the following three levels:

1. You don't understand.
2. You understand the ideas, information, or concepts intellectually.
3. You really get it. You understand at a deep, embodied, or visceral level.

The first level is fairly self-evident, so let's focus on the last two levels. One way to look at the second level would be that you could recite what you heard and know factually what it means. Many things in life are understood this way. An example is using directions to drive in an unfamiliar area. You might remember and be able to recite the instructions, but until you actually drive the roads and make the turns, you don't really know where you're going.

The third level could be described as being embodied—you know it in your bones. Having lived in the Boston area for almost forty years, Ken would say he knows, in his bones, how to get around town.

So why mention this? So what?

If you have insight beyond the intellect and grasp how the mind works at this deeper level, it changes your life. Something shifts within you, clarity emerges, and you see life in a new way. We have no idea if or when this will happen for you. We simply know that it is possible.

And the results of your shift will propel you into a new way of being. This is what happened for Sandy.

Sandy remembers the first time she listened to Sydney Banks. "Listen" is too strong a word for it—she didn't actually hear much or grasp the message. Months later a shift happened for her.

As a twenty-something, I often found myself in states of dissatisfaction, worry, anxiety, and general unhappiness, all of which I would blame on my circumstances: the raise I didn't get, the boyfriend who forgot to call, the car that needed fixing, etc. When these things would happen and I got into a low place, my habit was to milk it for all it was worth. I'd sit in a dark room and listen to melancholy music and feel sorry for myself—like that helped!

One day, months after hearing Sydney Banks, I can't remember why, but I found myself in a very familiar state of despair. I went home and did my routine—I darkened the room and put on the sad music. At some point it crossed my mind that I was signed up for a woodworking class and the intro session began in thirty minutes. With all the willpower I could muster, I got in my car and headed to the class. I almost turned the car around when I pulled in, but a friend who was also taking the class spotted me in the parking lot. There was no turning back.

I remember entering the large woodworking shop at the community college with the weight of the world planted squarely on my shoulders. Then something surprising happened. After the three-hour class was over, I walked out of the building and I was stunned by the brilliant, star-filled night. I realized that I felt great! What happened? Not one circumstance in my life had changed, and yet I felt great.

In that moment, I understood for the very first time, and without intellectual effort, the connection between my thinking and my feeling and experience. Back at home in my low-mood routine, I was convinced that I felt bad because of certain things about my life or about me. Outside the woodworking class, I had the same life and I was the same person, yet I felt wonderful. The only thing that had changed was my thinking, but that turned out to be the key. It was the beginning of my journey of understanding how my mind works.

What a difference an insight makes.

There is a Feeling to It

When you understand something at a deeper level, your sense of knowing often has a feeling component to it. People describe such a feeling in different ways:

- A feeling in your gut
- A sense of rightness in your mind
- A feeling in your heart
- A quiet knowing that goes beyond the intellect

One of our clients recently described this experience as "being connected to my soul."

No matter how you experience a deeper understanding of something, there is usually a feeling associated with it. Increased understanding is a natural function that occurs effortlessly and automatically whenever your mind is open. It is like swallowing and digesting. You put something in your mouth, such as a drink of water, and the body simply takes care of the rest. There is no end to how deeply you can realize or explore your own inner human nature.

We hope you will look for these kinds of feelings as you read the book. You may have an internal sense of being centered, or grounded, or connected to something inside. You may describe it as having a sense of clarity, strength, or confidence.

Understanding Something Invisible

Understanding how your perceptions and feelings are generated each moment via thought is one of the most valuable insights you will ever have, yet it is easy to miss altogether. Even if you realize how it works, it is still easy to forget.

You may be aware of how your perceptions and feelings are generated in some moments but not in others:

- One day, you might have a new attitude about someone and realize you misjudged him or her. For a brief moment you may consider how a new thought—an insight—can change your world.
- You realize you were wrong during an argument and momentarily appreciate how your thinking misled you.
- You may get irritated by someone's behavior but later realize he/she was actually trying to help. You see you were in a bad frame of mind and apologize. For a moment you see the power of your moods is in your thoughts.

But those moments of recognizing the role of thought in your life are fleeting, if they even register at all. Most of the time, you assume you see reality objectively. Your thinking does not appear to have anything to do with what you experience and feel.

If you are like most people, you flit back and forth between:

- Seeing that your perceptions are coming from your thinking.
- Believing that you see life objectively.

In other words, you live in an alternating understanding about how your mind works. Sometimes you know your perspective is just that: a perspective created in your own mind; the next moment, you think you know how life **really is**. You can move along a spectrum from humility on one end to being quite arrogant and righteous on the other.

The creative process does not actually flit back and forth. You experience thought brought to life through consciousness at every moment in time. This is the only way it can happen. Your mind doesn't change from being a creative generator to a movie camera. It just looks that way because **your thinking makes it look this way**.

Can you see how invisible thought can be, while also being the central power creating your experience of life?

It's like magic: now you see it, and then you don't.

The Truth Will Set You Free

When you understand at the third level—the level of an insight— that your mind works only one way and is designed to function effectively, your system naturally heads back towards balance. All the brilliant, natural functions and associated capacities that account for you being at your best come back online more fully.

The moment you realize that you are only at the mercy of your thinking and nothing else, the thinking that you have been caught up in begins to loosen, and your mind becomes free of those feelings and perceptions. Without reactive thinking going on, you regain your balance. Your wisdom, common sense, and insight ability come back online.

Frank, a client of Ken's, is a lawyer who witnessed a memorable scene at the courthouse during a murder trial. The defending attorney grilled a woman on the witness stand who testified that the defendant had shot her son to death right before her eyes a few weeks earlier.

The attorney was trying to discredit the woman and was being rather unkind in the process. Surprisingly, the woman on the witness stand was calm, measured, and very clear. She was also respectful and responsive, despite the attorney's unpleasantness.

At one point, as Frank described it, the attorney turned to the woman and asked, "How can you be so calm if you recently saw your son murdered, and here you are accusing the man of doing it?"

With dignity and a clear voice, she looked the attorney right in the eyes and said, "I couldn't breathe, I couldn't eat, I couldn't sleep, and I knew I would die if I couldn't move forward with my life. I have to finish raising my other children and I needed to find a way. I realized I needed to

> forgive this man for what he had done. I found it in myself
> to do so, and I calmed down. I can eat and sleep now. And
> I would like him to go to jail for the rest of his life."

This mother saw the power of her own mind. She spoke about forgiveness, but forgiveness might never have been real for her unless she saw she was suffering from her own thought and that it was possible for thoughts and feelings to change from within. Because they did change from within, she was able to move on.

No matter what you may have experienced, it is possible to get out from under the appearance that a past event, however tragic and horrifying, has dominion over your current experience.

It's That You Think, Not What You Think

In their years of extensive training in psychology, Ken and Sandy learned scores of theories and strategies to help people attend to, analyze, and change their thinking. In his many years as an executive, Robin learned dozens of strategies to improve people's thinking through management and leadership trainings. The focus of all these trainings, and the activities they propose, is oriented to dealing with what people think. As you know, trying to change people's thinking can often be like trying to drive a car when the emergency brake is on.

> It is not *what* you are thinking that matters, it's realizing *that*
> you are thinking, and that your creative process has the power,
> at any moment, to give you a life that is stable or troubled.

The invisible power of this understanding frees you from having to change your thinking purposefully through effort. If, in a moment of reactivity, you remember that you are a thinker who is living an inside→out experience, you will settle, and your thoughts will clear. Your knowledge of insight principles will come to your aid effortlessly and insightfully from within. It is amazing how easy it is to find new ways of being, new ways of interacting with others, and fresh insights to solve your biggest challenges when you look in a different direction—to the invisible power of thought.

Bottom line: the cards are stacked in your favor. As soon as you see this and your head clears, you will have presence of mind, perspective, and the insights that you need to move forward—whatever is going on, wherever you need to go.

Like gravity, the power of understanding is invisible and potent.

In Summary:

- The essence of what we are pointing to is incredibly valuable yet invisible and easy to forget.

- Understanding how your mind works is your best ally for keeping your mind healthy and clear.

- Trying to change what you think is not as powerful or helpful as understanding the invisible power of thought

PART TWO

Basic Implications

six

IMPLICATIONS, NOT APPLICATIONS

Y ou might be wondering, "So, how do I do this?"

In truth, you can't help doing it. The logic presented in this book describes the way the mind works, and it can't work any other way. Once you see the logic of how something works, it guides you. For example, you don't really "do" or "practice" gravity. You know that objects fall down and not up, and you factor this reliable outcome into your life.

So, too, there are conclusions you can draw from the logic of how your mind works. In other words, certain implications become apparent once you see the true nature of the system. When humanity realized that the earth was round, the concern about falling off the edge of the world no longer needed to be considered. When you have insights about the inside→out nature of experience, much of your illogical thinking about where your experience and feeling come from will begin to fall away.

There are implications to the false idea that the mind works from the outside→in as well. The table below contrasts the implications of how the mind works versus how the mind does not work.

How the Mind Works	How the Mind Does Not Work
Your experience is coming from your thinking in the moment (Inside→Out)	Your experience is coming from someplace other than your thinking (Outside→In)
A flow of thoughts is constantly available bringing with it insight and wisdom.	Lots of willful mental activity is required to fix life's problems
The power to create feelings and experiences is inside.	The power is in circumstances, events, and other people.
You feel your thinking.	You feel what is happening to you.
You experience a unique reality that comes only from your thinking.	You see an objective reality that everyone can see.
The present moment is the only time when experience happens.	The past and the future can affect your feelings and state of mind independent of your thinking in the present.

Before we dive in, however, we'd like to offer a distinction that may assist you in getting more out of the coming chapters.

Knowing Principles vs. Creating Rules

If you are like most people, your attention mainly focuses on your thoughts, ideas, hopes, desires, physical body, environment, goals, plans, and challenges. You move through the world with little attention to the living dynamics of your own human process.

As interesting as life is, we are pointing you toward understanding your amazing human system, which is operating behind the scenes at an invisible level. If you focus on how to apply what we are saying to find solutions or better strategies, you'll miss the opportunity to see the deeper implications of insight principles. Here are two examples:

1. You have an insight and are thrilled to come up with a new way to speak to your spouse or coworker about a touchy subject. You love your new thought and find relief when your new action produces a better result. You might think to yourself, "I must remember to do it this way, every time, from now on." You don't stop and reflect on the brilliance of your innate capacity to see life anew with new thinking. Instead of trusting that you will have more insight about communication in the future, you make up a rule in your mind about how to behave.

2. You work too hard and get wound up with tension. Then you relax and begin to feel better. Your mind clears, your perspective opens up, and you have warmer feelings for the people around you. Instead of being grateful for your innate design and seeing the role of thought in your inner life, you look around and wonder what to hold responsible for your better feelings. You decide it was the lunch you just had at a new restaurant. Before you know it, you are having meals at that restaurant on a regular basis.

It is so easy and commonplace to forget that you are experiencing life within your own mental creative process. As you go forward into Part II of the book, the danger is that you will start to look for ways to solve your personal or business problems with what you read and stop looking in the direction of your innate mental functions that are operating behind the scenes.

This is not a book of **prescriptions** for what you should do or how to live better. It is a book of **descriptions** of the phenomenally brilliant design of your mind and how that design plays out in life.

We hope this next part, as well as the whole book, will deepen your understanding of your human operating system and take much of the hard work out of personal development. These chapters will explore the implications of insight principles with a view to helping you see more deeply the inside→out nature of the human experience and the brilliance of its basic design.

In Summary:

- You can't "do" the principles.
- You can easily forget to look behind the scenes and see the logic behind how your mind works.
- Understanding implications is more fruitful than adopting fixed rules.

seven

INSIGHT—YOU CAN HAVE NEW THINKING AT ANY TIME

"Never underestimate the power of an insight....
Sometimes an insight is worth all your
previous experiences in life put together."

~ Sydney Banks

A s a human process, insight is as natural in the mind as breath-ing is in the body. Insight is a constant possibility. In fact, you have insights all the time. Whenever you have new thinking and see something new, you are having an insight. You can't stop it from happening.

Insight is a living function within your mind, operating independently of your voluntary thinking.

Insight is the Real Mother of Invention

There is a deep intelligence that runs the mind that is the mother of insight. This mother is your greatest ally and resource in life. Insight can be more a part of your life, no matter the circumstances.

The second time Michael Santos went to prison, he went as a volunteer. He had recently finished twenty-six years in prison for trafficking cocaine, and he went back as an inspirational speaker to help inmates in the San Francisco prison system.

Michael has written seven books on prison life and the criminal justice system. He earned a bachelor's and a master's degree, and started a doctorate, while incarcerated. He has taught classes at Stanford, UC Berkeley, and numerous other colleges. His classes are favorites in the criminal justice programs, and students cram the seats and floors to hear him speak. He now aims to inspire others to break through expectations and reach their highest potential in prison. Michael's vision is to transform the prison system from a warehouse for humans to a place of healing and empowerment.

Soon after he entered prison the first time, Michael had a huge insight for himself. "I was twenty-three years old when I came across a philosophy book that others had buried in a box beneath some metal stairs at the Pierce County Jail. At the time, I didn't know what philosophy meant, but I flipped through the pages, trying to learn. When I came across the story of Socrates, I knew that I found a source of inspiration. The story I read described Socrates' imprisonment, and told the story of how he responded to the death penalty imposed upon him. Rather than running away from his troubles, Socrates spoke about the importance of facing struggle with dignity.

"After reading the story of Socrates, I made a commitment to face the challenges of my life with dignity. That approach inspired me to find or create steps I could take to reconcile with society. At the time, I didn't know what it would mean to reconcile with society, but days of contemplation led me to project what law-abiding citizens would expect from a man in prison."

While others might see prison as the end of their lives, Michael realized that he had the option of preparing himself for a life after prison. Even though his "life" appeared to be decades away, Michael saw that he had a great self-development opportunity in front of him. For Michael, this was energizing and inspiring.

Since his release, Michael has devoted himself to sharing his insight and helping inmates see their time in prison in a new way. This is a fulfilling and worthwhile mission for him. However, the power in his story, and the truth about people, is that everyone (including inmates) can have an insight *for themselves*. Only insight can change the way life looks to you.

When an insight occurs within your mind, as it did with Michael, the world as you know it changes. The change can be subtle or powerful, but either way, your reality shifts. It shifts because your thinking shifts.

An insight can show you things that you hadn't seen before. It is as if something new has come alive in you.

Sandy saw this for herself when she had an insight about worrying. Sandy grew up in a family of world-class worriers. She didn't know her parents worried or that she had picked up the habit. It seemed normal to feel anxiety before entering new situations, before events (both happy and sad), and before traveling. To her, thinking ahead about all that could go wrong was a mark of maturity and responsibility.

For several years after learning about insight principles, I continued to worry. Then one day, while dining with a friend, I was laying out my plans and contingency plans for my upcoming vacation. "Wow, you are a worrier," my friend remarked.

I was really surprised. I didn't think of myself as a worrier, just a good planner. And I told her so. She responded, "Then how come you seem so anxious?"

After dinner, I just couldn't get the conversation out of my mind. I do tend to overplan and think a lot about the what-ifs and the what-could-go-wrongs. I found myself beginning to wonder if that was worry. And if so, so what?

Some time later, I was once again doing my "thinking ahead" about an event, and I really noticed the feeling that went along with that thinking. It wasn't pleasant. And then it hit me: I'm worrying! I could feel the anxiety of my planning efforts for the first time, and I did not like it.

This was Sandy's first insight about her chronic worrying. What felt normal and expected to her suddenly felt odd and optional. Soon after this insight, it began to look ridiculous that she should think ahead about events in ways that lowered her spirits. Worry went from being beneficial and necessary thinking to looking like a complete waste of time to her. Planning was fine; it was the worry that was optional.

With insight, your new reality will seem fresh. A new direction appears that gives you energy to move forward when you feel stuck.

Your world can change at any moment with insight.

The Power of Insight in Business

We have worked with countless teams that had insurmountable earnings targets, ten-year-old multibillion dollar asset allocation problems, or had to shut down a 900-person site due to a failing business.

These teams encountered almost every conceivable problem, but the moment they knew to look in the direction of insight, they were able to move the issue forward, sometimes with miraculous results.

Is this luck? The right circumstances? We have observed this phenomenon for more than fifteen years, in countless situations. When a team uncovers an insight, its view of the situation changes, and the solution emerges.

Here is a story very similar to a number of other teams we have worked with:

> "Everyone told me to keep the closure of the plant a
> secret until the last possible moment. Otherwise, I'd have a

massive loss of the workforce before the fulfillment of our final contracts, which were going to last about one year." This was Brian, the owner and CEO of a recreational equipment business. A downturn in sales was necessitating the closing of one of his manufacturing centers, resulting in the layoff of more than 150 people. "I felt bad enough about the layoff, it just didn't seem right to keep people in the dark and then shut the plant with no warning.

"I had had my own coaching in insight principles, so I trusted that an answer would come. Eventually, I had the most interesting insight: why not share with the employees at the plant what I had learned about how the mind works? I would be honest with them about the pending closure, but I would also expose them to some pretty great information."

Brian spoke to his employees, explaining the plan to close the facility at the conclusion of their current contracts. He asked them to stay on as long as they could, and he requested that each of them attend a program to help prepare them for the year ahead. We worked with Brian's crew in groups of twenty-five, sharing insight principles.

When the groups came to the training, they were worried and upset. They thought they were going to go through a superficial, inspirational course to get them excited about staying. The acrimony and distrust was palpable. We explained that we were only there to help in a difficult situation and that we wanted to share what had been helpful to us in challenging times. As the plant employees began to hear the logic of how the mind works, their hard feelings subsided, and their fear turned to curiosity about what new ideas might show up. Most had considerable insights that buoyed their spirits and oriented them to be creative, both for themselves and the company.

About twenty people left the company within the first month of the announcement, which was considerably less than was expected. To Brian's surprise, the team that remained was able to fulfill the orders in less than six months.

"Our new efficiency allowed us to restructure our pricing," Brian told us a few months later. "New contracts followed, and the plant was never shuttered. We were able to keep most of those who stayed on. To this day, the esprit de corps and creativity of the site exceeds what it was before the incident occurred. I am so glad we took the route we did."

You are, quite simply, an insight-making machine! As a kid, you were constantly learning via insight. Constantly. This is how you learned to speak and get along with the other two-legged creatures in your home. Without insight, learning would never happen.

The beauty of insight is that it is tailored by the deeper intelligence within you for the challenges you face. It integrates your knowledge and is sensitive to your situation and what is relevant and important to you. It shows you what you need in such a way that you can intimately understand it. This kind of specialized answer to your challenges can only come from within—from your own wisdom and innate intelligence.

Insight on Demand?

Not exactly. The potential for insight is always present. It is a constant, natural function operating behind the scenes, but you do not control when or how it comes. However, you can stifle it, in the same way that you can suppress the function of your immune system.

When you were young, it was easy to learn a language, get over things, play with enthusiasm and abandon, and learn new skills. The flow of creative thinking from your core was new and fresh. That core is where insight comes from.

You have a core of creative energy hardwired into you, and it is your most brilliant source of solutions. There have been times you looked to this core when faced with a challenge. However, because most of your education and training encourages you to look to your mental storehouse of models, strategies, and solutions, you can overlook this resource.

Jim Collins, in his book *Good to Great*, made the astute observation that contentment with being good is the enemy of reaching to be great. Being good, he suggests, can keep you from striving for more innovation and excellence. We've noticed that this can easily become your habit when you get comfortable working without a flow of insight.

> **One of the greatest enemies of insight is attachment to figuring things out using what you already know.**

Have you ever been vexed by a problem that is in your area of expertise, only to have some newcomer solve it? How come someone with little experience can have such innovative perspective? You can probably guess the answer.

Here's a story from Robin's consulting days that shows how insight came to his aid in a surprising way:

90

We'd been hired by the Executive Committee of one of the largest companies in the industry we served to help their CEO, Joe, make up his mind. In short, the company had invented a breakthrough technology for a business that they had divested years earlier due to underperformance. They had three options: reenter the business, license the technology, or simply sell it. Despite a clear financial assessment, they could not decide, primarily because of Joe's indecision. The divested business had been his first General Manager assignment. He just couldn't make up his mind. When we were contacted, this indecision had been going on for over a year.

After several months of preparation and reviews, we finally met with Joe to get him to decide. It took about twenty minutes to take Joe through the PowerPoint deck. With impeccable logic and clear prose, the case and various recommendations were obvious. As we finished the last slide, Joe looked up and asked me directly, "So, Robin, what should I do?" As I sat there and wondered about his question, I had an insight. It occurred to me that he did not really know what he wanted, so how could I answer his question? As I looked at Joe, I had another insight that just looked so obvious to me—that I should tell him just that.

So I did. Warmly, but directly, I said, "Joe, I can't answer your question because you don't really know what you want."

There was more than a pregnant pause in the room. I heard my boss, sitting to my left, breathe in rather quickly, and my words sort of hung there. Joe seemed to take them in and wondered for a moment. Then his eyes lit up and he answered, "You're right." He flipped over the presentation so we had some blank paper, and we proceeded to have an impromptu working session, covering all sorts *of aspects of the technology and the industry. As we casually kicked around ideas, Joe had his own insight: they should sell.*

We came out of the meeting as heroes.

As I reflect on this event with what I now know, I see what was behind what happened. In that moment with Joe, I was not caught up in any thoughts about who he was, who I was, or what was at stake. I was at home in myself, in balance, and in a relaxed feeling. I did not have to work to have insights; they came up without much fuss when needed.

*In contrast, if, as part of our preparation, we had **imagined** what Joe wanted, we would probably have come up with a complex and sophisticated logic pointing to a single solution, with the hope that it would sway him. Even more probable, we would have thought so hard about the whole situation that we mostly likely would never have guessed he would ask the question he did.*

Built into you is the capacity to have all the wisdom and insight that you will ever need. You don't need to think hard to resolve issues or question. You just need to know that this ability is in you and how it naturally presents itself.

From the Ordinary to the Extraordinary

Insight can be the most ordinary event. When you reflect on the menu at a new restaurant and just the right meal choice occurs to you, you are having insight. When you realize a hidden meaning or feeling behind what someone is saying, you are having insight. It happens all the time.

Insight can also strike deep and rock your sense of reality, as it did for Michael Santos when he realized he could use his time in prison to create a great life for himself. This also happened to the woman, mentioned earlier, testifying against her son's killer. She realized she could forgive him and continue to live her life fully.

Insight can become as ordinary as it was when you were young. The less burdened by outside→in misunderstanding, the clearer your mind is and the greater the flow of fresh thinking. It feels great to be in that insightful state of mind where creativity flows and you delight in life.

Insight is like a butterfly that you wish would light on your shoulder. It is possible that a butterfly might find you as you run around the room at full speed. It is far more likely to land on you, however, if you sit still.

Non-Stick Mind

You are always at a fork in the road, as we described in Chapter 1. You can work your thinking or look to the invisible power of thought behind what you are experiencing. Understanding the invisible power of how insight principles work through you is what creates psychological freedom. With that freedom, your mind will be more like a nonstick surface and less bogged down with extraneous thinking. It will be open, curious, and flowing with new thinking and perspectives.

As you read the following chapters on personal power, feelings, time, ego, stress, and other topics, go beyond what you already know and allow new insight from within. You never know how brilliant and transformative your own wisdom can be. In a moment of awareness and understanding, your intellect and knowledge are both present, right alongside your clarity, wisdom, and perspective. You will get the best of both worlds—the benefit of what you know and the latent power and potential of the deep capacity for wisdom and insight that lives inside you.

In Summary:

- Insight is a naturally occurring function of your mind.

- When insight occurs, it changes the world you live in from the inside.

- You do not control the function of insight, but you can interfere with it.

- The more you understand (remember) that this function is innate, the more you look in its direction and let it happen.

eight

THE POWER IS ALWAYS INSIDE

Walter is the finance professional for one of the businesses within a global construction company. As Walter liked to say, "I'm the tail on the business dog." In other words, his job is to cater to the needs of the business. For the most part, he does not make his schedule or set his deadlines. Whenever the business needs him, he must be ready.

While Walter loves his job, and he has been doing it for twenty years, he could not imagine doing it well without the chronic feelings of stress and pressure. "It's the nature of the job," he would say.

Along with the leadership team of the business he supports, Walter attended our Insight Synergy Program. Here's his account of the experience.

> At first I struggled with what you were telling me. Somehow I heard you saying that everything was my fault. I already knew that my attitude was important and that I controlled my attitude, but I didn't control what was happening to me. It wasn't my fault that a

business leader wanted a twenty-slide PowerPoint™ presentation tomorrow and I was already working overtime on two other projects!

As I kept listening to what you were saying, I finally realized that you were not talking about control. You were saying that the deadlines and business needs could not make me feel a certain way. Unless I thought about my work in a stressful way, I would not experience stress. The power is on the inside, because that is where the feeling is coming from. There is no power in the circumstances. I may not be able to control my thinking in the moment, but I can know that my thinking is the source of my experience. This has helped me see that my stressful thinking made no sense. Why continue to make myself feel badly?

When you understand how the mind works, you know that outside circumstances do not dictate how you feel or function mentally. This realization gives you psychological freedom.

Yes, there are many times when you will feel like a victim. When you forget how the mind works and entertain insecure thoughts, you will experience insecurity. If you are thinking you are a victim, you will feel like one. However, when you remember how your mind actually works, you will see the experience for what it is: insecure thought. Feeling victimized won't last if it looks like thinking. It is not possible for anything, other than your own thinking, to create a feeling.

When you see that your reality is created from the inside→out, you see that there is no power outside of your mind that can cause you to feel something.

> **Your experience from moment to moment
> is between you and you.**

Here is how a colleague of ours observed this truth in action.

George was asked to give a keynote address at a conference. Just as he took the podium, music began infiltrating the conference room. A Cinco de Mayo celebration, complete with a boisterous mariachi band, was commencing next door in the hotel ballroom. The entire conference audience was distracted by the music.

The conference staff who were called to help hustled next door to lower the volume, but mariachi music can only be played so quietly! We could tell George was flustered as he tried to regain the audience's attention. After five awkward minutes, he appeared to regain his composure. Shortly after, all eyes and ears were on him, and his talk was very well received.

After the talk, we asked him about his experience. He said, "When the music started and the audience got distracted, I lost my bearings. I could feel the anxiety move from the top of my head to the tip of my toes. I lost my momentum. Then it occurred to me that my anxious feeling was coming from my thinking and not from the room full of distracted people. I settled down and delivered my talk as if I was hanging out with my friends in my living room."

In the midst of an important moment, George realized that the power was inside him, as it always is.

Is it Always Inside⟶Out?

We can hear your objections.

"What if someone threatens me, my family, or my job? Won't I experience fear?"

You might. We are not saying you won't experience something. We are simply pointing to the source of that experience.

This book is not about what you should or should not experience, but about how experience happens.

What you experience comes from your thinking, at any moment, and from nothing else.

If you thought the person threatening you was joking, you might feel amused. If you did not understand why they were threatening you, you might become curious. If you thought they seemed troubled, you might feel concern for them. There are thousands of possibilities, and whatever you happen to think, for whatever reason, is what you will experience.

When Ken taught insight principles in the Suffolk County Jail in Boston, there were often many angry men railing at the cops who had arrested them or at the correctional officers for the treatment they received. During the classes that usually lasted ten weeks, one by one the men settled down and got perspective on their experiences from the inside→out.

One day Jimmy, in for his second time, raised his hand in class and said, "You know, I was asking for it, selling drugs to whoever came by. I have been angry with the undercover cop since I got busted. He was just doing his job. It was me who screwed up."

By the end of the class, Jimmy was even feeling sorry for how hard the job must be for the corrections officers who have to deal with so many angry inmates.

Realizing that the power is always in your mind can also generate what looks like miracles in business.

We recently worked with the leadership team of a large division of a major global conglomerate. This team was beginning the process of restructuring. This restructuring would involve selling or joint venturing the parts of the division that were no longer critical or strategic. As a result, many on the team and in the organization would leave the company or lose their jobs. Uncertainty was high. Insecure feelings were growing by the day.

When they began to recognize their worries as thoughts being created from the inside→out, they individually and collectively calmed down. They began to see that they would all be OK, one way or another, and that they could help others realize this too. Instead of being worried, they began to feel empowered to do their best for each other and the company. The compassion for people was palpable and would help when the time came for the changes to be announced.

Within four weeks of the program, the parent company decided to dramatically accelerate the restructuring. The parent company also decided to effectively dissolve the entire division and reassign the remaining parts to other business groups. This was a surprise to the team, and within two weeks they had to pull together a major review of their business, six months ahead of schedule.

"As we went through this process," remarked Clarence, the general manager in charge of the restructuring team, "we were surprised how relaxed we felt. We witnessed bad behavior in the other businesses, but we didn't let it get to us. Surprisingly, we laughed a lot!"

Although the end result was not what they wanted, collectively or individually, they saw their own role in the experience of it. Staying centered was possible, and they felt a whole lot better than they would have otherwise.

By the end of the following quarter, the division posted its best financial result ever. In the face of tough circumstances, the team exceeded what everyone thought possible.

As this example shows, there will always be circumstances that require your response. If you understand that being human is an inside→out endeavor, you can maintain your balance while thinking and acting effectively. You will have a stream of intelligent thoughts and will know how to deal with the situation in useful ways. You will feel a graceful sense of empowerment and confidence.

**Can you remember a time you were challenged but
kept your bearings and acted wisely in a surprising way?**

⁂
⁂
⁂

Sometimes, you simply forget where the power is.

In Summary:

- Your mind is designed with the power on the inside. It is within you.

- Experiencing such freedom happens when you understand the invisible power of thought.

- When you remember where the power is, you are free to receive the insightful, effective thinking you need.

nine

YOUR FEELINGS ARE
WHAT YOU THINK

There is a fallacy at play in your life. It asserts that outside influences cause your inner feelings. This is a misunderstanding of how the mind works. It is a very common misunderstanding, given the way life appears. It really looks as if:

- You are angry because your plane is delayed.
- You are hurt because of what she said.
- Being in the woods makes you serene.

None of this is accurate. So what *is* happening?

You Feel Your Thinking

Without thought, there would be no feeling. You cannot be grateful or full of love without grateful and loving thoughts. You cannot be afraid without fearful thinking.

Here's an example of what happened to Sandy; you may have experienced something similar.

One evening, I walked into my house and saw something move. Knowing none of my family was at home, I thought there was a stranger in my house. I immediately became afraid.

The next moment, I realized it was only a shadow moving on the wall from a branch swaying in the wind outside, and no one else was in the house. My feeling immediately changed to calm.

How did that change happen? The shadow did not create fear or calm. Sandy's thinking did it in both cases.

Movies, TV shows, newspapers, novels, song lyrics, etc., reinforce the perception that feelings are caused by external events, and that certain things are always wonderful and others are always sad or stressful. We often hear people at work saying that if only they had a different boss, a different job, a different workload, they could relax and have a better life.

However, someone in the next cubicle—working for the same boss, doing the same job with an even bigger workload—may be energized, challenged, and able to rise to the task with joie de vivre. One person experiencing the loss of a loved one may feel grief and despair while another may feel gratitude for time spent together. One moment, you may worry that the glass is half empty and feel you lack adequate time, energy, or resources. An hour later, it's more than half full, and you may have a deeply peaceful feeling about your life, grateful for the abundance and opportunity ahead.

You Don't "Do" Your Feelings

Let's cover what we are not saying. We are not implying that you are consciously or deliberately thinking your feelings into being. We are simply pointing to the fact that it is your mind forming the thinking that is experienced as feelings. Realizing this fact is incredibly powerful and useful.

Nor are we saying that you can control your thinking or your feelings. Thoughts and feelings occur so immediately that they are impossible to stop. It's like trying to stop a sneeze or a muscle spasm. You can be in a feeling state without even understanding the thinking that brought you there. When thoughts arise, there is an instantaneous emotion or feeling.

We are also not saying that feelings are unrelated to people and circumstances. The core of empathy is to sense and understand the feelings of others, or to see the importance of events in the context of what is important to others. This is part of your natural emotional intelligence as well and a crucial component of healthy, successful relationships.

Here is an example of the empathy that evolves when you understand that you feel your thinking.

A group of engineers from a defense contractor had the unenviable task of meeting with their military customers about technology they had designed which was failing in the field. The customers were irate and used all the words and body language you can imagine to express their displeasure.

The engineers felt uncomfortable, but thanks to their grasp of insight principles, they realized their feelings about the military customer's behavior were the result of their own thinking, and not the barrage from the customer. They knew that they needed to remain focused and deeply listen to get the information they needed to fix the problems.

The engineers also realized that their customers' thinking was on display in the form of upset feelings. The engineers could see that behind all the yelling and threats lay a genuine concern for the end user of the technology: the soldier. So they didn't take what was happening personally. The engineers felt empathy for the customer, and this ultimately helped defuse a volatile situation.

The engineers didn't "do" empathic feelings; they simply experienced their thoughts as feelings.

Feelings Happen in a Flash

The fact that you experience a feeling directly after an external event makes it look as if that outside event caused your inner feeling. The internal creative process is so fast and invisible, you don't see it happening.

Just as in a dream, you create and perceive reality instantaneously. Whatever reality you dream up in the moment will have a feeling component to it—this is what it means to be human.

Misunderstanding how the mind works leads many people to incorrectly assume the immediacy and intensity of their feelings justifies dwelling on negative reactions and acting them out. It certainly seems as if the stronger you feel something, the more real and true your perspective is! But this is not how it works.

You have strong feelings because you have strong thoughts that seem real to you. Just like Robin.

*After a long day of meetings, I arrived at the airport. It had
been a busy week, and I was looking forward to getting home.
In fact, a little snooze on the plane sounded perfect. By the time
I got to the gate, there was no one else waiting to board. As I
handed over my boarding pass, I noticed I was seated in the last
row—the row just in front of the toilets, with seats that do not
recline. "Oh, well," I thought, "so much for that nap!"*

*Imagine my relief when I entered the plane and found it half
empty. I approached the flight attendant and asked to move seats.
With a rather cold and slightly strange look, she asked me for my
seat number. I told her. Then she replied, "So what's the problem?"*

*I explained to her why I wanted to move seats. She asked
for my seat assignment again. Now I was beginning to feel a
bit irritated. This didn't look complicated to me, and she really
wasn't being helpful. I patiently repeated my seat number, to
which she snapped back the same response as before—the equivalent of "You're not moving your seat, Mister!"*

*You can imagine my reaction. One minute I was happy to
be in a half-empty plane, the next my blood was starting to boil.
A flood of thinking came in with all the associated feeling: "She
shouldn't be treating me like this! I'm a customer. I have a full-
price ticket ..." In that moment, my understanding of insight
principles was forgotten, and if you had asked me why I was
upset, I would not have said that my thinking was causing my
own reaction. It really looked like it was the flight attendant.*

*As the feeling got worse and I contemplated a host of reactive
strategies (call the airline's CEO, ask for her name, get the people
around me to weigh in), the intensity of the feeling seemed to alert*

me to what might be going on. Out of the corner of my aware-
ness, I just barely remembered that we can only feel what we
think, and the flight attendant's behavior was not the cause of my
upset. Despite the upset, I had the thought that the situation was
not heading in a good direction. This was quickly followed by the
recollection of what they now do to people who argue on planes!

As I started to remember that the only cause of my upset had
to be my thinking, despite the apparent nature of the circum-
stances, it seemed to make sense to back off and chill out. With
all the dignity and restraint that I could muster, I picked up my
bags and made my way to the back of the plane. I was still both-
ered, but I was remembering once again how the mind works.

How instantly and simultaneously thought, perception, and feeling happen in your consciousness! This is your inner creative process, and without it you would not experience anything. When you realize this fact, even unwanted feelings you've had for decades can dissolve. These feelings, like all feelings, are generated by your own thinking and can disappear in an instant.

Neuropsychologists and medical professionals emphasize the roles of the brain, the body, and your hormones in how you feel and how you think. We wholeheartedly agree that physiology plays a role in your sensations. Yet it is thought that brings your attention to them (or ignores or blocks them out), and it is thought that determines what you make of them.

A light touch from a loved one can feel wonderful, while the same touch from a loved one during an argument could feel (physically and emotionally) quite different. An itch on your neck will feel one way when you come out of a sauna and very differently when you are sitting outside wondering if there are mosquitoes around.

The Intelligence of the System

The mind can only work one way, from the inside→out. That means your feelings can only be coming from one place: within your own mind. Rather than looking outside to justify or validate your feelings, understanding insight principles lets you look inside, like Robin did, and remember that you are feeling your thinking.

> **Part of the intelligence built in to the human mind is that we feel our thinking.**

When you understand that your feelings are an integral part of your beautifully designed, intelligent human operating system, you naturally orient your inner life to healthier, more enjoyable feelings. Rather than thinking you have to change your life to feel better, you begin to see that you are designed to feel better and that it is natural to do so. It feels good to know that the power of your life comes from within and you are not the victim of outside situations. You relax and experience a flow of insight that brings you new solutions and hope—even in the most difficult situation.

Your Indicator Light

Since so much of your thinking occurs invisibly in the background, your awareness of your feelings can act as an indicator, letting you know what is happening within. Much like a car has indicator lights on the dashboard to alert you to the status of your engine, your feelings clue you into your internal psychological functioning.

This is a brilliant part of your design. Knowing that the invisible power of thought is creating your feelings allows you to tell, in the moment, whether you are in balance or not.

Feeling reactive and at the mercy of your circumstances? Your feelings are simply telling you that you have fallen into the common misunderstanding that your experience is caused by the external world. Got a positive feeling? That's your thinking, too, even though it looks like a promotion or winning the lottery did it.

Avoiding Regret

How many mistakes have you made when reacting to someone or to an event that you believed was causing you to be upset?

Here's a story describing what happened to one of our clients.

Julie's boss called her into his office and gave her a verbal tongue lashing for something she did not do. He was angry, claiming she disparaged his reputation, and the team's, with her behavior. Julie had no idea what her boss was talking about, but she could tell he was too upset to hear her out.

Julie was initially stunned by her boss's comments, but she regained her bearings quickly, realizing that her feelings were coming from her thinking. She did some investigating and discovered that her boss had misheard a comment from another team leader and entirely misinterpreted events. When Julie returned to her boss's office to correct the story, she was surprised that her boss remained angry—with her!

> In spite of having the facts at hand, it took her boss
> some time to let go of his thinking and the feeling that
> went with it. Such is the power of thought.

Julie's boss had no idea that his thinking drove his feelings and behaviors, let alone that his thinking was not accurate. If he had considered that his feelings were coming from his thinking and an indication that he may not be seeing the whole picture, he may have inquired with Julie about her actions and avoided a messy situation.

Your thinking will always seem real to you.
Unless, of course, you see that it is just thinking.

The power of thought coupled with the power of consciousness is a force to be reckoned with. You can't prevent your thinking from looking real to you and producing feelings that are sometimes quite strong. It's like putting a tea bag into a cup of boiling water. Once the tea and water meet, the water will be infused with the tea. The longer you leave the teabag in the water, the stronger the tea gets. You can't stop it.

Seeing that you are feeling your thinking enables you to step back and consider the source. You can then decide to act on your thinking and perceptions or to wait until your perspective shifts with new insight. A fresh feeling can indicate that you have more wisdom; when you have more wisdom, your actions will likely produce a better result.

In Summary:

- You feel your thinking. Your feelings are created within your mind via the gift of thought.
- The creative process happens so fast and invisibly that it appears your feelings are caused by events and circumstances, even though it can't work that way.
- Feelings are part of the intelligence of the human operating system. They are moment-to-moment indicators of what is going on within your mind.
- The strength of your feelings is NOT an indication of how well they represent objective truth.
- Realizing how your mind creates your feelings can facilitate living in more and more healthy, positive feelings.

SEPARATE REALITIES

Have you ever been completely astounded, or at least surprised, by what another person does or says? Perhaps you found yourself wondering, "How the heck could they have done that?"

How about the reverse? Have you ever been challenged by someone who couldn't understand why you did something, and yet it was obvious to you?

Sometimes you wonder what on earth we humans are thinking …

It was almost New Year's, and the house was full. Robin's cousin was visiting, and the kitchen had been a whirl of activity all day. All that was needed was to clean up. The traditional chicken soup was almost done. Long hours of simmering were over, the flavoring bones and vegetables had been removed, and the delicious soup was cooling, waiting for the fat to be skimmed.

As the five-gallon pot sat on the countertop, cousin Lee, thinking she was helping with cleanup duties, marched over,

grabbed both handles, took it over to the sink, and emptied
the contents down the drain! She saw a pot full of murky
liquid and assumed (thought) that it was the water left over
from boiling vegetables and needed to be thrown out.

You can imagine the consternation that followed.
The cry, "What were you thinking?" rang in the air.

By this point in the book, you are starting to understand how the mind
works. You are seeing that you are living in an experience—a reality—
that is crafted by your own thoughts and that this process is invisible. If
you see this is always happening in you, it logically follows that the same
phenomenon is happening in everyone on earth. Including cousin Lee.

But wait, don't we all think the same?

If we did, we would all be having exactly the same experience, and
the example of Robin's cousin would never happen. While you may
have similar or overlapping thoughts with others on some things,
you just cannot see or experience things the same way, unless you
have exactly the same thoughts.

You don't have to look too far to see that everyone lives in separate realities. Given that this is true, your world is literally different and could never
be the same as anyone else's.

This implication of how the mind works is ordinary but profound. We
think we are seeing the same movie in the theater as our family member
sitting next to us but are surprised to hear what they tell someone else about
it afterwards. We believe we have communicated well to our colleagues or
team and are flabbergasted when they go off and do something contrary to
what we were asking or suggesting. The list could go on endlessly.

Stop for a moment and consider just how different the world is for your spouse or a good friend. It is usually more different that we can even imagine.

Hard to Remember, Easy to Forget

The invisible nature of the creative process can make this tricky to remember. Since your mind makes the world look so real, it does not look like your thinking is creating your experience. As a result, you forget you are a thinker and therefore also forget that everybody else is too. A good example of this happened a few years ago.

We were working with a business team of ten people. We were on the third day of our program, and everyone was seeing these principles to a greater or lesser extent. As we often do, we had the team begin working through a business problem to experience how different their work could be in light of what they had just learned about the human mind.

After about an hour, the feeling in the group had gone quite flat. The conversation was not really progressing, but everyone was trying to be polite about the lack of progress. We stopped the group and asked them what was going on, using this new understanding as the lens.

As they started to reflect and discuss, one person asked a tentative but very powerful question: "Given that we all live in separate realities, are we all having the same conversation?" The group took turns sharing what they thought the conversation was about. As each person spoke, it became increasingly clear that they had been having ten completely different conversations. They were all shocked!

We greatly underestimate how different other people's worlds are.

When you understand separate realities, it becomes obvious that others will not think like you do or see things exactly the way you see them. We have noticed that when people realize this, other people's thinking, feelings, and experiences become more interesting.

If you like to travel, think for a moment about what it is like when you visit another city or country on a holiday. You see differences everywhere you look. Isn't that why you travel to new places? You are curious. You are genuinely interested.

When you begin to see how people operate in separate realities, you find yourself being interested. You listen more and communicate more effectively because you make fewer assumptions.

You are also more likely to look for the wisdom in others. Rather than honing in on how others are agreeing or disagreeing with you, you might wonder, "What are they seeing that I do not see?" Without effort on your part, you find you've put your own reality aside in order to better see another's. Learning about the world of another enriches your experience.

Seeing Innocence and Forgiving

A powerful implication of how your mind works is the fact that you do what makes sense to you in the moment—based on what you are thinking in the moment. You can get lost in your thinking and act unwisely from time to time. So does everyone else. Sometimes there's only soup broth at stake, and sometimes there are very serious consequences.

We all work in the same way. Everyone can operate from an outside→in misunderstanding and get caught up in reactive thinking some of the time. In that ignorance, we all innocently act on what seems true in that moment, without realizing our thoughts and actions may be neither wise nor humane.

If you see someone's negative actions with an understanding of how their mind works, forgiveness becomes a viable option. Not because you condone, but because you see that everyone does their best, given what they are thinking.

One of our colleagues, Gary, was developing a new practice in the Houston area, running workshops and trainings along with his therapy and consulting practice. One of the women who participated in his trainings, Mary, began to make subtle but disparaging remarks about him. She was also developing her work in that local area, and it appeared that she wanted to take clients away from Gary's new practice.

117

When Gary found out, he felt betrayed and enraged that someone he cared for was doing this to him. He was so angry and upset that it was hard for him to focus on his work and teaching, much less get enough sleep. His stress was definitely getting the best of him.

Because Gary had been a student and teacher of insight principles for years, he knew his own reactions came from within. Gary hoped for an insight.

It took more than a week, but one day, as he was unlocking his car door, it hit him that Mary's actions somehow made sense to her. He remembered her troubled past and her difficulty with relationships. Gary realized that Mary was just completely caught up in her own world. His heart went out to her for the life she must be living.

In that moment, Gary realized that Mary's actions were not personal. She didn't really know him very well. With that insight, his upset began to fade and he began to relax.

Within an hour or so, he had more insights. Although his hardest feelings were subsiding, he still felt disturbed about the effect on his reputation. He also knew that to go on a campaign against Mary wouldn't do any good, nor would it get him over his own reactions. In fact, it would only make things worse. Eventually, he discovered that very little came of the incident in regard to his practice or his reputation.

Gary never mentioned any of his experiences or insights to Mary. Seeing the innocence of the situation, he found it easy to forgive. However, he was careful regarding any professional contact he had with Mary from then on. Today, he can be friendly and cordial with her within the professional community they share.

There is no end to how deeply you can realize that others live in a world much different from your own. Even the people who are closest to you, whom you know best, live in a different reality—a reality more different than you will ever fathom.

In Summary:

- You will always underestimate the power of the mental creative process in generating your experience and everyone's experiences from within.
- You have your unique thinking, and hence you live in a very distinct and different reality from others.
- Realizing this fact results in more humility, better listening, the option of forgiveness, and a keen interest in the wisdom within other people.

eleven

THERE IS NO TIME LIKE THE PRESENT

People like us, who believe in physics,
know that the distinction between past, present,
and future is only a stubbornly persistent illusion."

~ Albert Einstein

Do you ever notice how tense you can get when you are reacting to something in the past or worrying about something coming up in the future, all while trying to get some work done?

Have you ever gone to a show or an event and, even though you were there physically, you weren't present in your experience? While the actors were on the stage or the band was playing, your thoughts were focused on something else—maybe on work or a personal situation. Did the physical world vanish? Maybe this has happened while reading this book. You suddenly notice you don't know what you just read and you have to go back and read the page again.

Given what you now know about the mind, you can see that your experience does not come from your circumstances. It comes from your thinking. Let's explore another implication of this fact.

Lost in Thought?

Your mind can make it appear that you are in one of three places: the past, the present, or the future. But, if you think about it, only the present moment truly exists. You can be fully in your life, experiencing it as it is happening in the present, or you can be distracted, missing the action.

There is no past other than what you think it to be, and, similarly, there is no future. Now is really all there is. You cannot be anywhere else, unless you are lost in thought, and that can only happen in the present moment as well.

Your imagination, the creative theater of your mind, has such fabulous special effects capabilities that you can imagine future events as if they are really going to happen. If you are a worrier (like Sandy was) and you consider your worries for a moment—how much of what you worry about ever happens? Yet you experience the fear and anxiety as if they are happening in the present moment.

Similarly, memories come into your mind and create movies of past events as if they are happening again. Yet each time you revisit a memory, it is a little different. The thoughts that recreate the event in your mind will always be a little bit different. Sometimes a lot different!

Your experiences of the past and future are much like watching movies or television. They are dreams temporarily created in your imagination.

There certainly is value in reviewing events so you can learn from them. There is value in envisioning and having foresight to plan and implement your goals and desires. There is also great enjoyment to be had from your imagination. If you don't like getting stuck in traffic, you can think about an upcoming event and have a nice feeling while waiting for the traffic to move.

On the other hand, if you don't realize that you are experiencing your world through your thinking, your imagination can get the best of you. Let's look at two of the most common forms of this: worry and rehashing the past.

To Worry or Not To Worry, That is the Question

Is it nobler to endure the slings and arrows of a worried mind in service of preventing calamity, or is it wiser to have a little foresight, plan ahead, and then enjoy the moment?

Worriers spend a lot of time thinking it is noble to do the former. Worriers have a great deal more unhappiness and stress than is ever warranted. When you forget where your feelings of worry come from, it seems compelling to worry.

If you are a worrier, it is likely that you have the feeling of mild to moderate fear most of the time. It is so normal to feel this way that you don't even notice it. You always have something of concern on your mind. You might give yourself a break on vacation and let yourself enjoy the moment, but those times will feel like a break from reality, and you will soon find yourself returning to your worried thinking and feelings. You can feel good for a bit, but then you begin to worry that you are not worried, and you will seek something to focus on, reembedding yourself in your world of worried thinking.

It doesn't have to be this way.

When you worry, you forget what a resourceful and creative person you can be. You are not in the present moment and are not seeing your capacity for insight and responsiveness to life.

Here is Chad's story:

Chad was a thirty-year veteran engineer in a top leadership role in a large company. He had spent a great deal of his life in worry thinking and the feelings that come with it. He married someone who did the same. He and his wife worried about their three children, particularly their autistic son.

Chad's worry kept his mind busier and busier with the what-ifs and the what-could-go-wrongs. He was constantly sorting things in his head, both at work and at home. With all this on his mind, he became increasingly impatient and irritable.

Chad participated in a team program we conducted to help the leadership team of his organization deal with an upcoming restructuring. The restructuring would lead to the eventual dissolution of Chad's function. You can imagine the added worry about the uncertainty that was happening for Chad and his wife.

During the program, Chad began to see his habit of worry as a thinking habit. He began to catch himself reacting to the little nightmares he was creating. His awareness of the feeling of worry began to tip him off. Instead of dwelling on his fears and trying to strategize how to deal with them, he saw what they were—just thoughts. They began to subside. Then he realized something that surprised him: in spite of all the ups and downs, his life had always worked out. He and his wife had managed to find ways to deal with every challenge put in their path. In the absence of his chronic fear, and with a renewed confidence in his ability to deal with life, he began to relax and enjoy himself much more.

We did a follow-up call with Chad about a month and a half after his program, and this is what he had to say:

By the end of the program, I noticed the internal waters had calmed down. I have been able to maintain them since. It is very surprising. I am not as frazzled as before and quite peaceful. I am not being as affected by outside events as before. I see that it is just my thinking, and I have much more control over how I respond. Even though I have lots of balls in the air, I am dealing with stuff well.

In addition, Chad told us he has been sharing what he learned with his wife and oldest daughter, and he said the home front had settled down quite a bit too.

This is typical of what can happen as you learn about the invisible power creating your perceptions and the psychological freedom that comes from knowing this is the case. Of course, for some, getting over a lifelong habit of worry may be a longer, slower process. But with an understanding of thought and feelings, even the most entrenched worriers can find their way to a new lifestyle of greater ease, lightheartedness, and productivity.

Living in the Past

Dwelling on past hurts is another habit that takes us out of the present moment. One reason you might rehash a memory of an event is that you are troubled or bothered about something that previously happened. You want to sort it out or get over a disturbing aspect of the experience. You go over the event to find clarity or some logic that will help you come to peace in your mind.

While you are doing this, you most likely fail to realize that the way you felt about and experienced this event at the time was created in your own thinking. In addition, you most likely fail to realize that you are reexperiencing this event now through your own thinking as well. If you feel victimized or disempowered by someone, that feeling is created in your mind. If you feel depressed or disappointed by something that happened, those feelings are created in your thoughts now. How much of rehashing the past is just recycling old thinking?

This is not to say that other people are always acting with your best interests in mind or that life configures itself to your desires. But your experience of it, now and then, is what you make and made of it in your mind. As long as you are rehashing those feelings, you are unwittingly assigning the power of those experiences, not only to someone or something outside yourself, but also to someone or something outside yourself **in the past**.

As long as you try to solve pieces of your past experiences while they are framed by a misunderstanding of where your power and your feelings reside, you will spend more time and energy than is necessary. This unproductive state of mind and the suffering that accompanies it can persist for a very long time.

Sandy found herself sitting next to a woman on a plane who was experiencing precisely this kind of unproductive state of mind. Even though Sandy had a book in her hand that she was trying to read, her seatmate kept striking up conversation after conversation. We'll let Sandy tell you what happened.

> *It was December, and I remember the woman seated next to me was flying to spend the holidays with her son and daughter-in-law and her family. She shared a painful story of her last trip and how she was deeply hurt by a comment made by the mother of her daughter-in-law. For months since that hurtful remark, this woman ruminated on the remark, rehearsed conversations with herself that she wished she'd had then, and created scenarios about what she was going to say the next time she saw this woman. She was very obviously reexperiencing her hurt as she retold her story.*
>
> *Finally the woman asked me what I thought. I said, "You still seem to be very hurt."*
>
> *"I am hurt," the woman replied.*
>
> *I looked at her and said, "But the remark is not happening now." I continued, "Right now you are on a plane talking to me. Your daughter-in-law's mother isn't here. How come you are feeling badly now?" I asked.*
>
> *The woman smiled slightly and then got very quiet. She didn't answer my question, and she didn't say much for the rest of the flight. When the plane landed and I gathered up my belongings to deplane, the woman turned to me and simply said, "Thank you. I think I am going to have a much better holiday."*

Sandy can tell us what she said on that day, but we may never know what her seatmate actually heard. The truth (and the good news) is that you, or anyone, can have an insight and hear something new and fresh. In that moment you can remember that you are not powerless and you are not a victim.

**What happened in the past does not have to
rule your thoughts and feelings now.**

We are sure you know what it feels like when your mind clears and your spirits lift. You suddenly see your thoughts and the situation they represent with more perspective. You come back into the present moment.

The mind has built into it a natural ability to see thought for what it simply is and to come back into the present with perspective. With that perspective comes a healing mechanism for whatever remains unresolved and held in thought. You can liken it to your tears washing away dust from your eyes. It's just natural. This is the mechanism behind the phrase "time heals all wounds." It's not time that does the healing; it's the mind's natural ability to have new thinking.

In Summary:

- The present moment is the only moment that exists.
- Thinking chronically about the past or the future keeps your mind occupied and less open to insight that might actually help you.

- When you remember that it's all thought, your past and future thinking drops away, and you come back to the present moment.
- Your mind has a natural built-in mechanism for insight and resolution that can heal whatever may be held in your mind.

PART THREE

Personal Implications

twelve

CHANGING FROM THE INSIDE→OUT

"Change—real change—comes from the inside out."

~ Stephen Covey

The self-improvement industry and literature is full of strategies, practices, and techniques to analyze your shortcomings and help you change your thinking and behavior to become a better person. Self-improvement is not the point of this book, though significant change in your inner well-being and outer success is likely if you realize the truth, for yourself, of insight principles and their implications.

The point of this book is to show you the invisible power of your mind and the value of realizing this power. If you see what we are pointing to, you will naturally evolve from the inside→out.

When you know the facts about how your mental life is designed, a lot of guesswork, stress, techniques, and extra effort diminish. You realize it is not hard to be yourself, to get along with others, and to be effective. You understand that being in balance and feeling at home in yourself is who you are designed to be. Your personal habits change—shedding the ineffective, less enjoyable habits and developing new ones that produce the results you want. Ultimately your inner life and your outer professional abilities move into a fresh phase.

In Parts I and II of the book, we laid out a foundation of understanding using three core principles and outlined their profound implications. We shared many stories of the insights and transformations people and teams have experienced once they saw the deeper implications of the inside→out paradigm. In all those examples, people's old thinking fell away as they realized the nature of thought more deeply, and they had new insights that changed the way they viewed and approached their challenges.

In Part III we will focus on some of the stickiest aspects of your inner life that may seem hard to be free of: ego, stress, and time pressure. We also look at how realizing insight principles can accelerate your personal evolution and strengthen your resilience.

Realizing the inside→out paradigm can effect change in you quickly or slowly. You may find some aspects of your life evolve easily and some don't. We'll say more about this in the next chapter on Accelerated Evolution.

Effortless Change

We thought it useful, at this point, to describe an orientation to change that we have found enormously helpful. This orientation arose from insights we have had on our own journeys.

These insights may help you as you read the next few chapters so you don't fall into the common self-improvement mindset of trying to be someone other than who you are, or trying too hard to speed up your development. These are not techniques. Realizing the following points will orient you on how to use what you read in the rest of the book without making it hard work. We want to show you how to fish rather than give you fish.

1. Realize that it is possible to be in balance and have clarity at any time, no matter what.

This may sound like something to do, but we are not intending it that way.

While reading the first parts of this book, you may have recalled situations you faced when you performed beyond your expectations and your feelings and mood were more energized and positive than you thought the circumstances deserved. Perhaps you had a day when everything flowed and the music of your day was pleasant and productive. Without understanding how your mind worked, you probably blamed it on having less to do, having had a great cappuccino in the morning that got you off on the right foot, or something else.

As you read and understand how your mind works, you may now be having insights about how brilliantly you are designed to function regardless of what is going on around you.

> **Your design includes the capacity to have perspective and a productive experience of life, no matter what.**

Though you may get this intellectually or perhaps even deeper, it may not (and probably won't) completely eliminate your stickier mental habits

135

that create your inner stress and distress, lead to ineffective behaviors, and impact your productivity and relationships. However, the more clearly you realize that your healthy balance is always available, the easier it is to notice when you are reactive or off balance. It is easier to consider, in those moments, that the first problem you need to attend to is in your mind. This can be hard when your ego is involved, your feelings are strong, or you are convinced that your stress is coming from external factors. The more you see that it is all thought, the less it will grip you and the more options and choices you will have.

2. Realize the irreplaceable value of being in balance.

If you are like our clients, and us, the hardest thing for you to realize is that you might be completely wrong about something you are thinking, feeling, or perceiving.

> **The invisible power of thought will always be much stronger than you will ever realize when it comes to how you see or feel about your world.**

The deeper you realize that your feelings come from your thinking and that that thinking is the only thing that can take you out of balance, the more you come to know how valuable it is to remember how your mind works. Your understanding then heightens your sensitivity to your different thought habits so that you can let them pass and come back into balance. It then becomes logical to question whether your thoughts and feelings have gotten the best of you and you should chill out.

3. Realize that insight can solve the most challenging problems.

The more you realize that insight is always possible, and the power it can have to transform your world from within, the more you look for it and the less you grind on problems. You inner wisdom then becomes a consistent partner in your life.

Here's an example:

> One of our clients, Angela, had just been promoted to COO, and with the new title came twenty-five direct reports. On a follow-up call, Angela asked, with building tension in her voice, "How can I get more time?"

> Robin suggested they reflect together. He asked her what she was spending the most time on. She explained, "I have to meet with each of my twenty-five direct reports for an hour every month." When Robin asked her why, she replied, "I want to stay connected to them and to be helpful." As they reflected more together, it occurred to Robin to ask if every one of her people needed the same amount of help.

> Angela had an insight. Actually, most were doing great. Only about half of them needed a regular check-in. Angela was happy to stop the call at that point, having saved some twelve hours a month, but Robin had her hang on a bit longer.

> Robin asked if she ever saw the twelve or thirteen who might need help at other times. "Of course," she replied, "I'm in meetings with them all the time." This prompted the question: in her meetings, could she observe these people to see how they were doing?

The light bulb went off again. "I could observe my people in real time, and if they needed some help, I would then set up a meeting. It may not be necessary to meet with all of them for an hour every month."

As Robin began to ask another question, Angela piped in, "You know Robin, I am beginning to see your strategy. I think I can start doing this for myself. Thanks for helping me see I can always look for an insight on whatever I need to clear up."

The reflecting Robin and Angela did together only took ten minutes and saved Angela about twenty hours per month. Even more useful was the power of insight that Angela realized for herself.

The next few chapters address some of the areas our clients find quite challenging. With the above realizations in mind, you will see how logical it can be for your evolution to accelerate without great effort, given a clear understanding of how your mind works.

We won't make any claims or promises about how fast your evolution will be, but we are confident about the direction it will go.

In Summary:

- When you know the facts about how your mental life is designed, a lot of guesswork, stress, techniques, and extra effort diminish.
- Change from the inside→out happens when you realize:
    - It is possible to be in balance with mental clarity, no matter what.
    - Being in balance is incomparably valuable.
    - Insight can solve your most difficult challenges.

thirteen

YOUR ACCELERATED EVOLUTION

*"Throughout time, human beings have experienced
insights that spontaneously and completely changed
their behavior and their lives, bringing them happiness
they previously had thought impossible."*

~ Sydney Banks

As we have explained so far, realizing insight principles can enable you to live with increasing clarity and wisdom. With this clarity and wisdom, you will naturally learn and mature with heightened ease and grace, accelerating your personal and professional evolution.

You are designed to learn, grow, and mature. As you develop, you become increasingly able to take on more responsibility and account-ability. There are many well-established psychological and behavioral models for adult and leadership development. Courses based on these models prescribe how to behave in more effective ways. We are point-ing in a different direction.

Though it is useful to have road maps and role models available to guide you toward greater maturity and responsibility, without a clear mind and your innate wisdom available to you, your chances of effectively and gracefully using those road maps and role models are hit-and-miss. We have seen the realization of insight principles clear the path for development better and faster than anything else we have ever come across. Such realization will accelerate your evolution as well.

Feeling Your Way to a New Normal

People who have met Robin might find it hard to imagine that he ever had times when he could be quite pushy and demanding. He is a warm, easygoing person, and he has been this way his entire life—until you stepped in front of him in a line, blew off a promise, or did something that he deemed was unfair. Then Robin's evil twin would emerge. He would become righteous and angry until justice had been restored. Robin tells his story here of how he found a new "normal."

It did not matter to me if you were the innocent agent behind the counter of the airline who was bumping me off an overbooked flight or a person who inadvertently jumped ahead of me in line—any perceived injustice deserved my wrath.

However, as I began to have my own insights about the how the mind works, I started to see, and understand, that the only person upsetting Robin was Robin!

Given the typical remember-forget-remember pattern of learning insight principles, I continued for a time with my habitual reactions. Each time, however, the reaction diminished. The reaction felt more and more "off," like eating food that tasted bad. The reactions became less intense and shorter.

> *If you ask today, even my friends and family would say that my "fairness habit" is a thing of the past. If it makes an appearance (which it occasionally does) it is more like a niggle than an atom bomb.*

Interestingly, Robin never worked at eliminating his habit. As his understanding of insight principles grew, reacting to a bad feeling made less sense. In parallel, the underlying thinking that was behind the reaction came to mind less often.

He describes his evolution in the following way:

> *As I got used to living with more ease and inner balance, disturbing feelings felt worse than ever, and I tended to remember that they were the result of thought and nothing else. Without working on it, I moved toward good feelings, and that became normal.*

The remember-forget-remember-forget pattern is common in everyone we know who has ever learned about insight principles. One moment you see the inside→out nature of psychological life, the next moment you don't. Yet you know that only one is true and the time you spend dwelling on outside→in reactions greatly diminishes over time.

The more clearly you see the inside→out nature of psychological life, the faster you stop blaming anything outside you for your feelings. You see that the power to stay internally balanced is up to you. You know that wisdom and insight, along with good feelings, are just thoughts away. Stress and upset disturb you less, and it becomes normal to have richer, nicer feelings and to spend less time uncentered.

> **Your understanding functions like
> a self-correcting mechanism.**

Baby Steps and Giant Leaps

Insight can bring about a big shift in your mental life, or change can happen gradually through a series of insights over a longer period of time. With knowledge of how your mind works, you tend to have more of both happen.

Though it may not be an everyday occurrence, we, and many of our clients, have had whopper insights. To name just a few:

- Mark and his team from Chapter 1 had the insight that it was their thinking that limited their ability to shorten the production time, not the complexity of their product.

- Ken's psychotherapy practice was completely transformed when he saw that everyone is innately healthy and that if they saw the power of thought, they would get out of their own way. (Chapter 2)

- Sandy's insight about her worrying had a powerful, immediate impact on her life going forward. (Chapter 7).

- Walter from Chapter 8 realized that the power to make him feel stress lived on the inside and did not come from his work deadlines.

These examples point to a fabulous possibility. When you realize that you live in a world of thought, and you see that they are just thoughts, large chunks of your thinking can fall away. It is like being in a movie and realizing that it is just a movie. The entire chunk of perceptions, feelings, ideas, and strategies—the whole story—is just thought.

Even if your insight doesn't change things in one fell swoop, the knowledge of how the mind works evolves your way of life from within, and this has varying degrees of impact over time.

As you continue to have insights about the inside→out nature of experience, your learning curve will trend up over time and will likely have peaks and valleys. You'll remember where your experience comes from, and then you'll forget.

Even for those of us who have been looking in the direction of this invisible power for many years, we still have days where it seems as if we never learned anything. Sandy can still get caught up in worry, and Robin can get hot under the collar. Ken, though he knows it is not the most useful direction to look in, can get interested in why he is thinking what he is thinking and not just see it as thought. We will probably go to our graves with these habits somewhere in our minds, but the likelihood of them rearing up will be less and less.

And then there are days when we catch on even more deeply to something we thought we already understood. Even after many years of knowing and teaching these principles, we continue to have insights that have significant impact, allowing another batch of our less useful thinking to drop away. We have come to expect this, to relish it, and to have hope in it. This is the nature of the journey you are now on.

A Word of Caution

Having a more effective and enjoyable mental life is very common on this journey. Then you can forget and go back to your old thinking, which can feel really bad. When you forget about the inside→out nature of experience, you may find yourself back in habitual, unwanted feelings—feelings that you thought had left you for good once you had an insight. This can be disappointing and even discouraging. Don't worry. It's all just thought. The thoughts will fall away again when you remember how your mind works.

A few months after a program with us, one of our clients, Lucille, complained to us that she was feeling anxious and stressed again.

"Why is this so troubling?" we asked her.

"I have been feeling so much better, and now I feel worse than I did before we met," she said.

"Haven't the last few months been great?" we asked her.

"Yes. It has been wonderful, and the team is doing so much better as well. The team is settled and productive, and we have been having more fun."

"You feel worse than ever because you are more sensitive to feeling anxious and stressed than you were before. Before, you were numb to your feelings, pushing past them as if they were normal. Now you have less tolerance for those feelings," we responded.

Lucille saw the truth of what we said and settled down quickly. She had additional episodes of stress and anxiety, but as each one came she had more awareness of what was happening in her thinking. This allowed for insight that has deepened her clarity and understanding about the power of thought, in herself and in everyone in her team.

Everyone's journey or learning curve will be different. You cannot tell when an insight will hit. You can't predict when a habit of thinking that dominates your way of seeing life will fall away, leaving you with more ease and perspective.

You have evolved with invisible elegance and grace since you were born. You still are. This understanding can accelerate that evolution by clearing up much of what is in the way because of an outside→in misunderstanding of how the mind works.

In Summary:

- Realizing insight principles will accelerate the ways in which you naturally evolve and mature.
- Once you realize the inside→out nature of life, you will be on a learning curve that has peaks and valleys but trends upwards.
- As your awareness of the power of thought increases and your habits of thought drop away, you find your normal life has more clarity, perspective, humanity, insight, and good feeling in it.

fourteen

GETTING OVER YOURSELF: EGO REVISITED

Ruin and recovery are both from within.

~ Epictetus

You were born a thinker. You are free to think anything you wish, and one of the things you think a lot about is yourself. Much of the thinking you do about yourself, especially early in life, is invisible to you. Consider this story from Ken:

> When I was young, I grew to be 5'8" tall by the sixth grade. In my school, the children lined up by height to attend the monthly school assembly. I would always go to the back of the line with the tallest kids. I stopped growing at 5'8" but remained one of the tallest kids in my class for the next few years.

I never consciously thought much about my height. Then for high school graduation we were all asked to line up by height. I immediately moved to the end of the line with the tall students.

To my surprise, I heard the teacher in charge call out, "Hey, move forward!" I looked around and realized the teacher was talking to me. I began to move forward and ended up near the front of the line. I was dumbstruck. It never occurred to me that I was no longer one of the taller kids in school.

Unbeknownst to Ken, using the gift of thought, he had created a tall identity in the privacy of his mind. You, too, have been crafting a sense of self your whole life. You have been deciding what is vital and important to you and what you want and need in life to be secure and happy. Your parents helped. Parents will share their values and beliefs (thoughts). Parents will also observe you as you grow up and make statements like "this is my sensitive child," or "she is a tomboy," or "you look just like your father, and you are stubborn just like him," etc. Invisibly, this thinking becomes a reality in your mind. It no longer looks like thinking. It just looks true. These thoughts make up your ego.

Ego is, simply, thinking you have about yourself.

It is mostly invisible, habitual, and running in the background all the time.

Neither Bad nor Good

The fact that you have thinking about yourself is neither good nor bad. Without an understanding of how experience gets created from the inside→out, however, you can easily find yourself on very tenuous psychological footing. When you become strongly attached to the thinking you have about yourself, you are locking yourself in a mental bind, even when the thinking is positive. Seeing the thinking you have about yourself for what it is (just thinking) frees you from the grip of believing the thinking to be reality.

Let's say you see yourself as someone who is decisive and who rarely makes mistakes. As long as this looks to you like your identity, you will want to defend this identity. It can become important to you to be decisive and right all the time and hard for you to admit when you don't know. You might push through decisions that are not fully thought through. There is a common and telling phrase for this. It's called "saving face." Much time and money gets wasted, and many opportunities get missed, when leaders act this way.

Without understanding the invisible power of thought, it's easy for the identity you created within your mind to appear as if it represents who you really are.

You can be the smartest person on your team and pride yourself on your ability to be brilliant. But if you attach your sense of worth to your brilliance, you'll have to keep showing everyone how smart you are. You can miss the wisdom in others and the opportunity to bring out the genius in your teammates.

You can be the most attractive person in the building and be delighted with the attention it might bring you. But if you attach your security to it, you'll be insecure each time you look in the mirror and notice that you are aging or that your tan is fading. You may fail to see the inner beauty that people exude when they are at home in themselves. Even worse, you may fail to see it in yourself.

Is it bad to be decisive and confident in your decisions or to be proud of your intelligence or appearance? Of course not. You can have a long list of attributes and values with which you identify. You are never going to be able to stop thinking about yourself, and we are not suggesting that you try. We want you to simply see for yourself that your thinking is the sole determinant of your feelings about yourself and about your life.

Ego vs. Humility?

Jim Collins, in his book *Good to Great*, shocked the business world in 2001 when he wrote that genuine personal humility is an essential quality of great leadership. Most people believed that leaders needed to be charismatic, larger-than-life figures with strong egos.

To us, humility is not the opposite of a strong ego. Humility is a natural outcome of seeing how the mind works. Humility arises when we see that everyone has wisdom and insight, that two or more heads are better than one, and that being in service to what is wise and wholesome works the best in the end.

As you grow in awareness and maturity, invisible and sticky ego thought habits become more visible and look less useful. It is then, and only then, that you can truly begin to let go of this thinking and lead with more genuine humility.

We describe these thought habits as sticky for the following reason: when you have thinking that blames external circumstances for your feelings, you feel justified in defending yourself and acting on those feelings. The stronger the thinking, the stronger the feelings become. Your ego thinking is most often developed with an outside→in misunderstanding, and you can take whatever is associated with that thinking very personally. As we pointed out in Chapter 8 on Feelings, the more strongly you feel something, the more real, or "sticky," it seems. Unless, of course, you understand how the mind works.

If you understand the power of your mind to make any thought seem real, this awareness alerts you when ego-thinking habits are taking over your mind and feelings. You realize that the thinking is interfering with your clarity, humanity, and common sense. You can back off to get more perspective.

You come to appreciate the wisdom and intelligence in yourself and others and the powerful forces within you that subtly bring you just the right insights to solve your hardest problems. With this humility, you find gratitude for the miracle of your own innate wisdom and the wisdom in others.

It is humbling to witness this power, unless you consider these gifts of nature to be your personal achievements. That would be your ego taking credit where credit is not due. You were not given complete control of your mind. You were, however, gifted with a mind that allows you to understand what is going on and to regain harmony via the design of the system.

What About Ambition?

Ambition is the strong desire to achieve a goal. It often comes with the sense that the achievement will do something for you, such as make you a better person or make you happy and fulfilled. This outside→in misunderstanding is fatally flawed.

Ambition can organize and motivate you toward a worthwhile achievement such as "I am going to be the best manager I can possibly be" or "I will bring this project in under budget and on time." Having a clear vision for what is possible is useful. Our natural creative energy then flows toward getting things done.

The rub comes when you think your inner sense of security and self-worth is connected to these outcomes. Then, whenever someone else shines or it looks like your goal is being thwarted, you may feel threatened. Instead of focusing on doing your best, you may subtly (or not so subtly) undermine others. Instead of being appropriately watchful of schedule and expenses, you push people, and mistakes are made.

We are not saying it is bad to be ambitious. We have a very ambitious company vision. We are committed to sharing insight principles with the entire world. We would love to see the world transformed by realizing the inside→out nature of human experience. We know how much peace and well-being will result. But we are not personally attached to the outcome in a way that disturbs our peace of mind or our sleep at night. We benefit from a strong desire to achieve our goal and, along with it, a flow of energy and insight from within.

Will I Lose My Passion?

Passion is a wonderful feeling. It is the natural flow of your creative energy from within. But it is a slippery slope when you think that the feeling of passion is driven by something external—getting what you want, doing things your way, or having others like you. If you attribute your passion to a boss you find inspiring or a project you love doing, you are missing the essential facts. You are, at your core, a creative soul, and passion springs from the life force within you.

Here is an example of how a misunderstanding of feelings and passion can play out. Let's say you are passionate about a project. At some point your initial enthusiasm and energy shifts to impatience and frustration. It looks like the reason for the shift in your feeling is a misstep, a delay, or something else about the project. Disappointment and/or disagreement arise, and you get off balance. From an unbalanced state, you are less open, less creative, and less capable of seeing viable options. Your energy drops, and you feel it's an imposition that you have to struggle in order to keep going.

Then, in a flash, if you remember where your feelings and experiences come from (inside and from your own thinking), you will see that your disappointment, impatience, and frustration are simply a mood to let pass. You see that you will soon come back to clarity. Insight can begin to flow again, heralding the return of your creative thinking and your passion.

A Little Understanding Goes a Long Way

Before we understood that the ego is just a collection of thoughts, we used to tackle our clients' egos head-on. We used to go to battle with their bad habits and bad behaviors. We would coach people on how to think in more mature ways. We would suggest more balanced and wholesome perspectives and attitudes to adopt. We would give suggestions about what to do differently and how to feel and be better interpersonally.

We were trying to replace one set of habits with habits we thought were better.

It was a lot of work.

Now we see that our clients simply misunderstand where their feelings are coming from.

Our goal is to help them see, as deeply as possible, the power of thought and the beauty of how the mind works.

Madeline is a young, high-potential leader in a Fortune 100 firm. For the initial years of her career, she was a highly effective individual contributor. Madeline is extremely bright, and she loves to solve puzzles—the more complex the better. It gave Madeline much pleasure to have a reputation in the company as the go-to person. In fact, all her life Madeline was at the center of the action.

When she was given her first assignment as a people leader, Madeline found herself in unfamiliar territory. Leading people was very different from her previous role. She felt overwhelmed and stressed. Her boss called her into his office and told her that her team was losing confidence in her. She looked so harried and rushed all the time that no one wanted to ask her questions or get her help. Consequently, the team was floundering.

Madeline asked her boss for advice, and he told her, "Always look like you are in charge and have everything under control."

"What if I don't?" Madeline asked.

"Then fake it," he said.

So Madeline developed a talent for looking calm and positive. Her husband would tease her because when he called her at work, she answered in her "office voice." He said she always sounded so upbeat.

Poor Madeline—this intense acting job took a toll. At the end of every day, she would virtually collapse in her car. She felt like a failure because she didn't know how to lead her team, and she felt like a phony acting as if she did.

Eventually Madeline saw the drama being created within for what it was. She recognized that the feelings of stress and pressure were thought-generated, and she saw the power of insight more clearly. She saw that not having all the answers was part of learning a new role. Acting as if she had all the answers was actually making her work harder. Maintaining a self-image is hard work!

"I couldn't believe what happened once I woke up to all my mental wrangling. I had expected to be an instant success as a people leader. When that didn't happen, I tried so hard to figure it out and make it work. It never occurred to me that it was a puzzle to solve. Puzzles were fun for me. I always approached them with enthusiasm and curiosity, and the ideas flowed. I love to reflect and let new ways of seeing things occur to me. I forgot to do that in my new role."

"The first thing I did, which seems so obvious to me now, was get to know my team. They were all unique and needed different guidance and direction. All but one were able to articulate how I could best help. The less articulate one was a more complex puzzle for me, so I am still sorting that out. What a relief to see that I don't have to know what I am doing every minute and I can take the time to see what ideas arise."

Understanding how your mind works will give you a new view of what the ego is. You can't lose your ego, but you can see the illusory nature of it. As a result, your ego thinking will dominate your day far less, and it will become increasingly normal for you to take yourself less seriously and enjoy a more productive life.

In Summary:

- Your ego is simply the thoughts you have about yourself, your needs, and your desires.
- Humility naturally results in the absence of ego thought habits.
- Your ambitions and insecurities will get the best of you if don't realize that your happiness and security are natural outcomes of your innate functioning.
- Understanding the nature of thought can relieve you of taking yourself too seriously and losing your bearings.

fifteen

A LIFE WITHOUT STRESS?

*Stress is nothing more than a socially
acceptable form of mental illness.*

~ Richard Carlson

Some myths stick around for centuries before they are finally debunked. We can think of three examples that are particularly striking. Luckily, two of them are now permanently consigned to the history books:

The earth is flat.

The sun revolves around the earth.

But the third is alive and well, and still being perpetuated throughout the civilized world: stress is caused by circumstances, events, and other people.

Here is Google's current definition of stress: "A state of mental or emotional strain or tension resulting from adverse or very demanding

157

circumstances." That would be a fairly commonly shared definition of the source of stress.

However, there is only one explanation for why you get stressed and stay stressed for periods of time—your stress is generated in your thoughts. You may forget this and blame circumstances, events, and people, but they are not where the stress is coming from.

As we have been describing throughout the book, you are bombarded by messages suggesting that your feelings (and everyone else's) are caused by your circumstances, past, present, and/or future. This constant drone, combined with your own history of believing that all feelings work this way, incline you to accept stress as inevitable.

Yet it doesn't work this way. Your feelings, moods, and level of stress or well-being are always the result of thought creating your experience from within.

Sometimes you will see this, sometimes you won't. When you see it, stress will not make sense as a state to hang out in. When you don't see it, you will find yourself reacting and creating a habit of stress.

Stress happens when you get tangled up in reaction (thinking) about things that seem out of your control. Here are some common examples:

- Events or circumstances don't work out your way.
- Deadlines seem impossible.
- People don't understand or cooperate.
- Family or personal issues are more than you can manage.
- Projects are not progressing and your responsibilities are increasing beyond your comfort zone.
- There is not enough time for everything that needs to get done.

Sound familiar?

> **It is not the situation that is out of control;
> it is your reactions.**

Is it normal to be stressed?

It will be normal to you if you think being stressed is a natural consequence of life. Normal for you is what you are used to and have accepted—without realizing that thinking is creating it in your own mind.

Is Stress Useful?

Robin interviewed a CEO who thought that stress is a good motivator. This CEO confidently described how he would put as much pressure as he could on his people until they would come close to breaking, then back off a tiny bit so they wouldn't. In his mind, this was optimum leadership.

This CEO is not the only one who believes you can scare people into their best work. There may be a grain of truth behind his approach. If you threaten people with adverse outcomes, they will generally do anything to avoid those outcomes. When you are afraid or stressed, those feelings will motivate you *if you think they are coming from your circumstances and not your thinking.*

Of course, there is a better way.

Stress is created in your thinking. This thinking clouds your mind with imaginings and fills your head, interfering with the natural ability to have perspective and make wise choices. Chronic stress can make you sick. Current medical research appears unequivocal about this.

If you live in an outside→in misunderstanding of human functioning, stress will seem normal and ordinary. It may even look useful. But the moment you realize that the source of stress is in your thinking, it loosens its grip on you. This also explains why threatening an adverse outcome just doesn't work on some people. The sooner you see this, the freer you will be to lead a healthier, happier, and more productive life.

Our clients report a significant reduction in the level of stress they experience. Some have said that circumstances and relationships that used to seem inherently stressful now look different. These clients report a flow of insights rising to meet the challenges they face. We are delighted it is no longer normal for them to feel high levels of stress. In fact, for many it has become normal to not have much stress at all.

Can I Really Change That Much?

Yes.

The more you realize the inside→out nature of your experiences, the more likely you will catch yourself overthinking or reacting to things that seem to get your goat. When you remember that you are a thinker, innocently creating your moment-by-moment experience, the extraneous thinking drops away, like a dream that you are waking up from.

Irene felt chronically stressed about her role, her performance, and her reputation within her company. She had recently been promoted to a very senior position. She was promoted because of her deep knowledge of her field and her ability to get very complex tasks done on time and to a high quality. In spite of all her talent, Irene also had emotional outbursts in meetings, sometimes culminating with her in tears. For her to be successful in her new role, she knew she had to get her emotions settled down.

Irene grew up in a family that went through much turmoil and strife. She became accustomed to a level of tension and struggle, believing it was normal and expected in life. When she wasn't struggling, Irene worried that there was some important factor she was missing. The feeling of stress was so normal to her that its absence felt strange.

Irene's outbursts in meetings were like a release of steam from an overheated radiator. The overheating was tension that built up prior to her executive meetings. It didn't take much challenge or disagreement from her peers before her thinking pushed her over the edge.

As Irene began to realize the nature of her inner operating system, it dawned on her that her lifetime of stress was a habit she had learned. If she didn't react to her thinking about all the things going on around her, she had all the common sense, intelligence, skill, knowledge, and experience needed to get the job done. Her confidence took a quantum leap, and any self-doubt that lingered began to fade.

As Irene's mind cleared, she began to notice her reactions to her competitive peers. With her new insights, she found effective ways to be strong and clear with those peers in surprisingly gracious and diplomatic ways.

When you understand that your feelings are an integral part of your beautifully designed, intelligent human system, you naturally orient your inner life to healthier, enjoyable feelings. It becomes more natural and normal for you to live in these feelings. Stress and tension are your signals that you have fallen into the misunderstanding that your security and well-being are at the mercy of your circumstances.

When you see that the power of your life comes from within and that you are not the victim of situations, you feel better. Rather than thinking you have to change your life to feel better, you begin to see that you are designed to feel better. It is natural to feel balanced within.

But It's My Responsibility to Solve My Problems Now

Sure. But being stressed gets in your way.

Some people love to solve very challenging problems. The harder the problem, the more fun it can be for them. They like to think hard, step back and reflect, think hard again, get insights, think some more, talk to others, and on and on. It can be rewarding and enjoyable.

Except when it's not.

If you push and grind in your thinking to the point of losing your inner balance and well-being, you will feel bad—*because you feel your thinking*. This stress is not happening because the problem is vexing, it's happening because of the thinking you are having. If you are feeling stress and you remember how your mind works, you naturally look for new thinking with a hopeful sense of expectancy.

In this example, Martin, a director of finance in a large health care company, is working very hard to solve an important problem amidst his stressful thinking. He's getting nowhere—until he remembers what he realized learning insight principles.

Martin was between a rock and a hard place. He was tasked with creating a new mind-set about finance in his division of the company. His problem was that neither his internal customers nor his peers had any interest in this culture change. All they wanted from Martin was the service of their financial needs.

Martin had a command-and-control leadership style and he was a highly regarded analytical problem solver. These well-honed skills were not helping him influence his customers or peers. He was experiencing a great deal of stress, and he knew he had to find another way.

After having some insights about how the mind works, Martin's stress level decreased considerably, but it eventually returned to its previous level. Martin knew his thinking had something to do with his stress. "I can clear my mind and relax. I can compartmentalize things and get away from the problem and feel better," Martin said. "But then when I think about things again, I go right back into the stress."

When the stress and tension returned, Martin reverted to his analytical problem-solving mode, trying to figure it all out. No satisfactory ideas came.

Ken reminded Martin that he could think about his problem when he was in a relaxed state and still remain connected and responsible. "Instead of going back into problem-solving thinking, trust that you can get an insight and reflect on the situation without trying to solve it. Relax with the awareness that you don't know the answer yet. Look for an insight to come. One will come along if you are clear and attentive. Sometimes you need to just get clear what you need an insight about," Ken continued.

"I guess I need an insight about what I need an insight about," said Martin, chuckling. But he got curious, and within a couple of minutes, he saw he needed new insight about how to get his boss involved. He felt much better.

There is nothing that you can think about in a stressed state of mind that you can't think about better when your mind is clear.

In Summary:

- Stress, like any other human feeling or experience, originates in your own thinking and nowhere else.
- It may seem normal to be stressed due to the misunderstanding about where stress comes from.
- You can live a healthy life with little or no stress, regardless of how complex, demanding, and challenging your workload and relationships may be.
- When things are challenging and complex, insight is a much more effective and efficient direction to look in than stressful analytical thinking.

sixteen

GOT TIME?

*How did it get so late so soon? It's night before
its afternoon. December is here before it's June.
My goodness how the time has flewn.
How did it get so late so soon?*

~ Dr. Seuss

Panic. Urgency. Impatience. How often do you feel pressured by time? How often do you feel there is just not enough time in the day? How often do you, or people you know, panic or react to time pressure and end up doing dumb things that have to be cleaned up later and cost more time?

As you become more aware of the invisible power of thought, you will realize that your mental stress about time is created in your thinking, *even though it looks like external circumstances are beyond your control.*

Not Enough Time

Time cannot pressure you. Only your own thinking can. Here's a story about how Miriam, an HR Director in a sporting goods company, finds her way through a frantic state of mind.

Miriam sat back at her desk and sighed. "This is crazy," she thought. "I'll never get it all done."

Over the past year, Miriam's team had been asked to do more and more with fewer resources and increased constraints. With a major deadline looming, Miriam had a to-do list a mile long, countless unread emails, a calendar full of meetings, and two direct reports who were in danger of burning out. She'd been spending increasing time at work lately and could feel the effects at home. As she contemplated the impossibility of meeting her deadline and what it would mean for her career if her team missed it, a familiar frantic feeling welled in her chest.

The feeling tipped her off. Miriam had been in an insight principles program, and she remembered that her rushed and overwhelmed feelings were coming from her thinking, not the massive amount of work she was tasked with. She remembered the inside→out nature of her thoughts and feelings.

Yes, she had a lot to get done. Yes, there were constraints. Yes, her team was overburdened. But suddenly, it seemed clear that panicking and feeling frantic was not going to help her get everything done.

Instead, for the first time, Miriam got curious. "Once I saw my reaction for what it was, I noticed I settled down. I wondered what I could do differently to help me be more productive."

From this place of balance, Miriam had a few insights. She shifted her priorities and saw how her team could simplify their efforts and get some rest. Immediately, she felt freer. She realized that although she had work to do, it wasn't necessary to feel burdened by it. The burdened feeling was optional.

Miriam's insight about the true nature of her experience and where it was coming from helped her mind clear. In turn, her spirits rose and she saw creative ways to help her team.

Miriam's understanding of insight principles did not make the work go away, nor did it diminish the importance of getting the job done and helping her team meet its deadline. However, Miriam's understanding allowed her mind to clear, and she regained her sense of power from inside. She could then approach the situation with more insight, creativity, and productivity.

Inside→Out Time

In contrast, do you ever feel like you have all the time in the world to be yourself or to get something done? It is a pleasure to work in this feeling. You may have this experience often, or rarely, or maybe never. Most of us go back and forth (without realizing it) between being rushed and relaxed about time. Going back and forth like this is like having two lives.

One life is caught up in a world of time pressure. The other is a life of freedom in which you can breathe and look around at what is happening in the moment. You might even feel a timeless love and joy of life.

Ken learned an early lesson about being in time.

> *When I was learning to play the piano, it was a challenge to learn the notes and get my fingers to do what they needed to. It was then a new challenge to play the rhythm in time with the flow of the piece. Even harder was learning to play duets with my dad. I had to learn to stay in time with the music and with my dad.*
>
> *When it all came together and flowed without effort, it was a great joy. And sometimes it even sounded really good! The music was more than the sum of the notes. The experience felt timeless. We could go on for hours.*
>
> *Then there were the days it wouldn't flow, and no matter how much effort my dad and I put into it, we wouldn't sync up, and there wasn't much music to be had. We were thinking a lot and trying hard. Our bodies would get tired and stiff, even if we'd only been playing for fifteen minutes or so.*

At the core of these alternating lives is the invisible power of thought. One moment you are living as if the external world makes you feel and act the way you do, and time is no longer on your side. The next moment you are living in a beautiful life that has all the time in it you need.

Living and Working in Time

We are not saying that time does not exist. If you are late for the airport, you will miss your flight. Work projects and home activities take time to complete. Deadlines are real. There is an endless supply of meetings, emails, projects to manage, and other people constantly giving you things to do. Without understanding that life is happening from the inside→out, it appears as if these circumstances create the time pressure you feel about them. This cannot be.

The great value of knowing that your experience of time is created inside you is that you can have your mental freedom, enjoy your life, and have the clarity to get done what you need to get done, regardless of what the clock says—just like Miriam in the example above, when she regained her inner balance. She stopped imagining time was her enemy, forcing her to be stressed; she relaxed, had a flow of insight, and found the joy of solving a tricky problem for herself and her team.

If you find yourself under pressure and thinking your circumstances are doing it to you, the moment you remember how the mind really works, you stop. You take a break or pause and regroup. Once in balance, you will see what is needed and where best to put your efforts.

Part of the brilliant design of the human mind is that the power is inside, not outside. Other people, piles of projects, or pressing deadlines do not have the power to throw you off balance. Once you realize this, you find yourself being more skillful at saying no to things or being clear when you are asked to do more than is realistic.

> Sandy interviewed a particularly harried executive prior to his leadership retreat. He was lamenting that his home life was suffering due to his work schedule.

Sandy asked him, "Why don't you work twenty hours a day?"

"That would be unreasonable," he replied.

"Do you decide what amount of time at work is reasonable?"

He hesitated and said, "I guess I do. It doesn't feel like my decision though."

It does not feel like his decision because his thinking was invisible to him, and yet it was running the show, bringing him the experience of not having choice or power.

There will be times when you may want to overextend yourself or reach for unlikely targets. When you understand the nature of experience, you find a balanced state and decide what is best to do in the moment with common sense, rather than anxiety.

With the awareness and understanding we describe, the music of your work life (and home life) will feel harmonious more of the time, and your results will significantly improve.

In Summary:

- Your experience of time is created in your mind from the inside→out.
- Perspective and insight are your keys to organizing your time and prioritizing what needs to get done.
- With an inside→out understanding of thought, you can live your life with mental freedom, enjoyment, and great productivity.

seventeen

THE BOUNCE-BACK FACTOR

The key to keeping your balance
is knowing when you've lost it.

~ Anon

Our dear friend Christian, who runs an Aikido dojo in Pennsylvania, told us an interesting story:

As part of his training, he had the opportunity to study with one of the grand masters of Aikido in Japan. During his trip, he saw this short, thin, elderly master deftly handle many larger, more muscular, younger attackers all at once until they were all down on the mat, with him still standing.

"How did you do that without ever losing your balance?" Christian asked.

"No," said the Aikido master. "I lost my balance all the time. I just got it back very quickly."

Christian's story is a physical example and metaphor for the natural way your mind is designed to work.

Resilience

Resilience is simply your capacity to return to your natural balance and clarity when you lose it.

Thought habits based on an outside→in misunderstanding can easily create reactions that disrupt your sense of balance and personal security. When reactive thinking subsides and your mind clears, your feelings and troubling perceptions clear. You find the power is inside, and a flow of insight returns.

The faster and more fully this happens, the more resilience you will have. Seeing the fallacy of an outside→in misunderstanding powerfully and quickly increases your resilience.

Winning When You Lose

Winning business in the defense industry is an interesting endeavor. Contractors bid on programs and then wait for the US government to decide which company wins the contract. Such was the case with one of our clients; we'll call them RDR Company.

RDR Company was excited about an upcoming bid opportunity, one deemed critical to the long-term success of their business. They assembled an A+ team, many of whom had an understanding of insight principles, to create a competitive bid to win the program. This team labored for months, working many long hours and late nights to submit a strong proposal. They were proud and hopeful about their chance for success.

However, the RDR team was not selected as the winning bidder. Instead, the US government customer awarded the contract to RDR's direct competitor. The RDR team was disappointed, but their understanding helped them keep their bearings. They lost the contract, but they knew their experience of the loss was coming from their thinking. Instead of dwelling on the situation and becoming frustrated or discouraged, they remained resilient and moved on.

A few weeks later, due to a technical submission error by the winning team, the customer reopened the contract and asked all contractors to resubmit proposals.

It is easy to imagine another outcome if the RDR team had engaged their disenchanted or discouraged thinking, pointed fingers for their failure to win the original bid, or became frustrated.

Instead, because their minds remained free and clear, they reassembled quickly and were hit with a rush of inspiration and creativity. More long hours and late nights ensued, and the inspired team improved their previous proposal and submitted an enhanced bid to the customer.

Their clarity paid off. They were selected as the prime contractor on the program, beating the original winning team and securing significant business for RDR.

Resilience can be very profitable. Keeping your bearings contributes to the bottom line in a big way.

You Don't "Do" Resilience

Understanding how the mind works does not prevent disappointment or discouragement. Sometimes life does not work out. Thinking happens and feelings follow. You don't choose to have bothered or unsatisfied thinking. If you see it as thinking, however, you can have a choice about what you do with it next. When you recognize the actual source of feeling, you don't have to wait for circumstances to change in order for your thinking and feeling to change.

> **Resilience is not something you do.**
> **Resilience is built into the design of the human mind.**

You have been getting over things since the day you were born. Even without an understanding of how your mind works, at many times in your life you simply saw the folly of holding onto to thinking about past events. You moved on because your thinking moved on.

The Hard Stuff

Tragedies befall us. This is a sad fact of life. We are not suggesting you could (or should) just get over it. We are pointing out the innate healing capacity in your mind, which works more easily and quickly when you understand the role of thought in how you feel and experience life.

Healing is sometimes a very slow process, and sometimes it isn't. Sometimes it seems simple and straightforward and at other times complicated and layered. Whatever process you may go through in grieving a loss or adjusting to a new reality, the essence of the process is ultimately a change in how you think about your situation.

Your ability to adapt to new realities is grounded in your openness to new thinking. If you understand that wisdom and insight are available to you, you will gracefully and gradually see the downside of holding onto sad or fearful thoughts. You then find that they are replaced by more joyful memories and compassion for others. This is a natural healing process, but it is without a timetable, and there is no right way.

To us, it has helped to be anchored in the knowledge that there is an inherent wisdom to the design of our human minds. This came to be a powerful and valuable aid for Ken when his father suddenly died of a heart attack on a tennis court some years ago.

My dad was one of my best friends in life. We were always close and could talk about almost anything. He was a deeply loving and compassionate soul, and I thought he would be a great grandpa for my kids. He died at seventy-two, just before we could let him know we were about to start a family.

The message on the phone machine we heard after arriving home from the restaurant for dinner one night was unmistakable. Though she didn't say why, my mom's tone of voice said it all as she asked me to call right away. After we heard the sad news, we packed a few things and jumped in the car. I was stunned and watched my mind going through hundreds of thoughts and scenarios on the three-hour drive to my mom's house.

Every day of the next week or so was a roller coaster ride, alternating between a deep sense of calm and presence and waves of sadness, shock, and grief (and a host of other feelings that defy description). In between those waves, I felt clear, calm, and balanced.

I was extremely grateful for my understanding of insight principles. As I was having disturbing feelings, I was able to be with them and let them pass through. It helped to know that they would run their course and new thoughts and feelings would follow.

It also helped to know that I am inherently designed to be resilient and feel calm, clear, and good. As a result, it felt normal to me to be balanced, helpful, and compassionate with my mom and my sister in between my waves of grieving. Without understanding how thought works, I could easily have thought it inappropriate to feel positive in the midst of grieving while others around me were suffering. In the past, I had thought I was supposed to be down and sad when hard things happened.

The waves of emotion continued for quite some time. Even to this day, almost twenty years later, they can happen. I am enormously grateful for the wonderful relationship I had with my dad. I am also enormously grateful to have learned how the mind is designed. This understanding has enabled me to experience that gratitude and appreciation much more than I would have otherwise.

As in Ken's case, an understanding of insight principles and the mind's innate design for resilience made a huge difference in how he experienced this event. We have been through similar losses with many of our clients, and this knowledge has made a world of difference in every case.

With resilience, your mind can do what it was designed to do. It can have new thinking that might result in healing from a loss, inventing a new product, seeing a new way of working with someone, or (as in this case of RDR) winning a lost proposal.

In Summary:

- Resilience is the capacity to come out from under reactive thoughts and feelings so that you can return to your natural balance and clarity.
- Your mind is designed to be resilient.
- Seeing that negative reactions are coming from your thinking allows you to have a different experience on the inside without having to wait for something to change on the outside.

PART FOUR

Interpersonal Implications

CONNECTION AND SYNERGY

When we try to pick out anything by itself,
we find it hitched to everything else in the universe.

⸱⸱ John Muir

At the most basic level, you are connected to every other human being on the planet.

When your mind is clear and wide open, you touch that connection with others. You might have a philosophical moment and see life in all its grandeur or have a feeling of love or camaraderie with those around you. You might feel your deep commitment to your children or compassion for the suffering of others. You might feel the loyalty of your teammates and the joy of working together toward a common end. These are natural feelings arising from within.

> **The feeling of connection is part of your design for success.**
> **It is not something you do; it is a natural experience that**
> **occurs when your mind is open and you let the world in.**

Synergy and Universal Connection

When you live with the realization of how your mind works, you see the possibility of connection more and more because you recognize two things:

- Everyone's mind works exactly the same way.
- Everyone is connected to a universal wisdom that they rely upon.

You may have had the fortunate experience of working on a team or with another individual when, together, you created something beyond what seemed likely or even possible. Along the way, perhaps you had major differences in strategy and execution. You may have debated or even argued. At some point, your personal thinking quieted and you listened. You discovered something new together. It was exhilarating.

Carol is a Global Product Leader for a biotechnology company. She came up with an innovative idea to increase market share and brought her PowerPoint presentation to the leadership team. Within minutes of starting her presentation, the CEO stopped her. She had said something that intrigued him, and he wanted to know more.

Carol described the next thirty minutes as the best of her professional career. She, her boss, and soon the entire leadership team moved into what she termed "a place of pure discovery." "It was as if we were all connected, all moving together like the current in a river. We kept building on one another's ideas until we came to an idea new to all of us."

Carol's experience is not unique to her, but it is also not common for her. The same might be true for you. You love the feeling of connection and respect the value of synergy, yet they seem illusive. Why is that?

You don't have more feelings of connection or experience of synergy with others because you misunderstand how your mind works. You fail to recognize that the thinking clouding your mind has caused it to shut down and block your natural openness and flow of insight. There are so many ideas competing in your mind for your attention. Then there are the times when you do realize you are not open, but you justify your stance. Ego thinking can be the culprit as you stubbornly hold onto what you pride yourself in already knowing. The result of all this mental noise is that you fail to see that others may have wisdom and insight or that you may see something new.

Fortunately, at any moment, the walls can come down and connection is possible once again.

Seeing the Wisdom in Others

You live in the feeling of your thinking. As this fact becomes alive for you, you see yourself and others as thinkers. What you think and what others think looks less gripping. It is easier to set aside your ideas. You notice common ground. You see the grain of truth, even in ideas that you do not agree with. And when you find that you cannot listen or take in another's point, you know that too. You register on the inner feeling or reaction that alerts you to the steel trap door shutting down your mind.

Barry, a vice president of engineering for a large, successful technology firm, attended an insight principles program and told us the following story of how his learning helped him get over his reactivity to see the wisdom in others.

Prior to Barry's realizations about how people's minds work, he was so committed to his own good ideas that it was difficult for him to listen to others. He was known for his brief meetings and strategy sessions. After all, Barry usually had all the answers.

The fact that everyone's mind only works one way—and is designed to work well—hit Barry like a ton of bricks. He had always had confidence in himself. He knew he had a gifted intellect and he trusted his instincts. Other people, not so much. When he began to see the universal wisdom and instinct in those around him, it humbled him, and he became more open.

Then, at a strategy session with his team, Barry's insight was put to the test. One of his direct reports proposed an idea that to Barry was "utterly ridiculous." Upon hearing what the guy said, Barry described having a strong visceral reaction: "I could barely keep myself in my chair and so I got up and started pacing." The team knew something was up, but Barry did not say a word.

After a couple of minutes, Barry's reaction subsided, and he sat down. "I knew I was reacting to my thinking, so I let it pass," he said. "Then I asked to hear the idea again. This time, I heard something different. Maybe the guy said it better the second time, or maybe not. What followed was a lively and productive discussion. I know the old me would have missed the value and wisdom in what he was saying."

When you see your reactions for what they are and settle down, connection with others is natural. You see the wisdom in what others say. This is true one-on-one and with a team.

Effortless Synergy

Team synergy allows groups to "leap tall buildings" and accomplish remarkable results. This synergy may look like a fortuitous alignment of stars and circumstances. However, when you understand how you function, you see that synergy is a natural and effortless outcome of human minds working as they are designed. Here's an example:

> The leader of the finance group for a large manufacturing company asked us to work with his team. Our preprogram interviews revealed a team that described themselves as dysfunctional. Years of grudges and relationship breakdowns, along with gossiping and complaining, took up valuable time on the job. Important information was not being shared because people avoided each other. Though they were professionally competent and effective in their work, their lives at work were not fun, and their efficiency was lower than it could be.
>
> We explained in our interviews that we would not be focusing on the past or the current problems the team was facing. Rather, we would be sharing basic principles about how the mind works. The team was both relieved and skeptical.
>
> During the four days of our program, there was considerable challenge and lively dialogue about our message. Nevertheless, several members of the team began to understand the way their minds worked and to see for themselves their inherent design for success. Their old attitudes and grudges looked like old movies playing in their minds and no longer seemed worthy of holding onto.

At one point we looked around the room and noticed people who had avoided each other for a decade having lighthearted and insightful conversations. The feeling in the group was warm and collegial. The collaboration, humor, and energy to work together were tangible. The compassion for each other's shortcomings and foibles was palpable. In an amazingly short period of time, the team created a new set of values by which to live and work together that has held strong to this day.

We have a period of offsite follow-up after our team-building work to help participants deepen and strengthen the learning. Interestingly, Linda, one of the four managers in the group, made the following comment to us during a follow-up meeting: "Most everyone on the team is doing fine. It is like a new chapter for the department. We are helping each other keep our understanding fresh and top of mind. There are a couple of us that didn't seem to fully hear what you were teaching us and are still inclined to complain about their teammates. We do our best to ignore it and sometimes mention it to them. But we are not affected by it anymore. It doesn't take up much time like it used to. And it seems to be tapering off."

To the team and its leader, it looked like a miracle had happened. To us, it looked like a logical result of people finding a clear and accurate understanding of insight principles and the human operating system.

Your Brother's Keeper

The truth is, you are more like other people than you are different. Your humanity precedes your personality. As your understanding of how the mind works deepens, you catch yourself putting artificial barriers between you and other people. "We are all in this together" becomes more than a slogan.

We have several colleagues whose life's work is to take this principled explanation of the human mind into jails and prisons. The results have been astonishing. A remarkable conversation among inmates in a Santa Clara County, California jail, all of whom were incarcerated for serious felonies, was captured on video.

There were ten inmates, dressed in prison jumpsuits and covered in tattoos, discussing how they could help the corrections officers who guarded them. This is a sample of what they said.

"Please picture this," said one animated inmate. "What if all the officers in this jail took this class and they found the calmness, the control over their thoughts and emotions? Over the anger and stress. 'Ya know what I mean? Over all this frustration. And we could have this unity. What if they got the same thing? Do you know how many problems it would eliminate? The stereotyping. Venting frustration. And all the stress from home coming here."

Another young man shared, "They bring work home and they bring home to work ... so they're all messed up when they come in."

"Remember, we used to bring the street to the jail, 'ya know," said a third, "now we have something to help us and I'm willing to share it."

The inmates, who have had profound insights into how the human mind works, have transformed from being combative with the corrections officers to more relaxed and cooperative. They sincerely and compassionately expressed hope that the officers could receive the same education in order to find their peace of mind. Even without a reciprocal connection, these inmates felt empathy for the officers, many of whom had been rough with them in the past.

We have found that a shift reliably happens in people when they realize there is a universal wisdom and humanity built into everyone's inner life. They then find it difficult to be consciously unkind or unfair, to be greedy, to hate. Feeling connected to others and being willing and able to find synergies with others becomes a lifestyle.

We are not meaning to take a radical position or to prescribe a way you should or should not be. We have simply noticed these results of understanding.

In Summary:

- When your mind is free and open, you feel a sense of connection with others, and synergy becomes not only possible, but likely.
- Your humanity and goodwill emerge as you realize that you are just like everyone else.

nineteen

COMMUNICATION THAT REALLY WORKS

*The single biggest problem in communication
is the illusion that it has taken place.*

~ George Bernard Shaw

Perhaps this will sound familiar to you:

> "Some days he is so easy to talk to. On other days, I feel like I am hitting my head against a brick wall!" complained Amanda, one of our executive clients, describing her conversations with the CEO. Amanda had a long history of being angry and rebellious, which she attributed to a long history of unfair treatment by her family and others. She had toned down her anger a bit and, for the most part, she was more seriously bothered than outright angry while at work. However, bother as a lifestyle was getting the best of her.

We like to have our clients do leadership retreats (one-on-one intensive learning programs at our training center). A retreat is an opportunity to disconnect from ordinary distractions and see the logic of the principles deeply. At her retreat, it took Amanda a number of conversations over a few days to begin to see that her anger and bother were truly the product of her thinking and not coming from anything that was happening in that moment or in the past. She saw for herself that being frustrated and blaming it on others was just a mindset and not useful to indulge anymore.

As a result of her realization, she began to see her communication with her boss differently.

"I would get really frustrated on those days, but now I am seeing there is an art to getting through to him. It is a mixture of awareness of my own balance and seeing how open and clear he is—both in what he is thinking and in how he is hearing what I am saying. My reactions, which were a part of the problem, are so much less now because I see they are coming from my thinking." She continued, "I am not stressed anymore when I have to address issues with him, and the work is flowing so much more easily now."

The "art" our client is referring to is the fact that one moment you are free to entertain new thinking, and the next moment you are caught up in a set of thoughts and don't realize it. This dynamic (dipping in and out of realizing the power of thought) determines when communicating is effective and when it is not.

> **The greatest inefficiency in business is the ineffectiveness of communication.**

Communication works well when you and others are free to entertain new thinking. This happens when you and others are balanced, open, and in a good feeling. Insight will flow, and new understanding will happen effortlessly. Your knowledge and perspective are then broadened and enhanced. It is a joy to communicate this way.

Knowing the invisible power of thought is your key to maintaining effective communication. It enables you to see that:

1. Everyone's thinking looks as real to him or her as yours does to you.

2. A new perspective (insight) is possible at any time.

3. Your feeling is your best barometer for what shape you are in to communicate effectively.

Here's an example of how John, a senior executive for a global manufacturer in the electronics industry, learned to eliminate much of the ordinary noise and clutter in communication that often makes business inefficient:

John had been working on a joint venture (JV) for almost two years. He told us, "My idea is to use the Insight Synergy Program off-site to begin the planning process for the next level of engagement."

But John's team had concerns. "We are feeling pushed into a decision without adequate due diligence," they told us during our preparation interviews. "This is a decision with potentially significant negative ramifications. John has people coming to the off-site to start the integration process. We are not ready for that."

This discrepancy in views was problematic, so we suggested they speak with John before the off-site. As a result, John learned that others on the team had doubts about the joint venture.

As we started the program, John and others on the team were already on the defensive. There were lots of busy minds in the room. We spent the first part of the off-site focusing on the nature of thought and the freedom that comes when you realize that you are creating your world from the inside→out. When people have this realization, they detach from the thinking they brought into the room. They slow down mentally and become more present and relaxed. Humor, humility, and goodwill tend to arise. This is exactly what happened for John and his team.

When we entered into the business topics, some of the tension reappeared. A few noticed how easy it was to forget what they had learned about their thinking, and commented on it. This helped ease the tension and allowed the feeling in the team to stay open and curious.

As he reflected on what he had heard from the others, John sensed the team's concern as well as their goodwill. He saw that his team members were not diminishing his work; they were simply trying to protect the company. With considerable maturity and balance, John was the first to break the ice when the topic of the JV came up. He felt safe enough to be vulnerable with the team and shared how difficult it was for him to have worked so hard on something that the group was not fully behind.

"If you all think the JV is a bad idea, I can let go of it altogether," he started. He wanted to let them know that he was open for discussion regardless of the outcome.

The team felt respected and understood, and were touched by his humanity. They responded with care. "Thanks, John," said Marianne. "We were worried this was going to be a battle just to discuss it. We are not ready to start the integration process because we don't know if it will be good for the company to do the JV at all."

After some lengthy exploration of what had recently been discovered, John explained his deeper thoughts on the matter. "The only way to truly assess the risks we have been discussing is to start the integration process and see if the savings and benefits will really be there."

"Perfect," commented four of the team members, finally realizing John's logic and the wisdom behind it. Collectively, they hammered out a new go/no go decision tree. They also saw how to move things forward as John had suggested.

In the end, the team came into alignment, but more importantly, they had an experience of effective communication beyond what any of them thought possible. A few months later, they decided not to pursue the JV. Though disappointed, they were greatly relieved they had taken their trust and communication to a much higher level.

As If Their Thinking Doesn't Matter

Have you ever witnessed a scene like the following? A traveler in a foreign country is trying to have a conversation with a person who does not speak his language. Sensing he is not being understood, the traveler speaks louder—as if raising his voice will somehow make his words more intelligible.

As a witness to this common interaction, you can see the folly of it. Too often, however, when you are the traveler in the scenario, you believe you will get your message across if you simply say it louder or repeat yourself several times.

The same problem exists in your office and at home. How many times have you tried to share an idea with someone, only to find out they didn't understand what you were saying, even if it was for the umpteenth time? How many times have you asked one of your kids to do something and it just never happens?

We often fail to realize that people, including those closest to us, live in separate realities, where even the same words can mean very different things. We rarely check in with them to make sure we are communicating effectively.

One day Ken had just such a conversation with wife, Kailia.

> *I was home one Tuesday writing a document for a client when Kailia came in to talk. I paused what I was doing for a moment and she said, "I'd like to go to the mall and do some clothes shopping on Saturday morning."*
>
> *I said, "Great."*
>
> *At 10 a.m. on Saturday morning, Kailia came looking for me just as I was getting ready to go out to the yard to do some work.*

She beckoned to me, "Let's go," with delighted anticipation.

"Go where?" I asked.

When Kailia had mentioned the trip to the mall to me on Tuesday, it never occurred to me she wanted me to come along. I thought, "Great! Kailia will go shopping and I'll get some things done in the yard."

It is so easy to forget that realities are crafted by thought, not external circumstances. It is even easier to forget how different our realities are from one person to the next, even when we are communicating in what appears to be the same language!

The Busy Mind Factor

Even with a strong understanding of the power of thought, it is easy to fall into miscommunicating. Every communication has, at minimum, a speaker and a listener. The first opportunity for failed communication happens when the speaker thinks one thing but says another. How often have words come out of your mouth the wrong way? This is especially true when the speaker has a lot of thinking filling his or her head.

Then there is the listener who is hearing, not what the speaker is saying, but what he or she thinks the speaker is saying. Again, if the listener has too much thinking on his or her mind, the likelihood of this happening goes up.

And of course all bets are off when both are busy minded.

Here's a common example of how communication goes badly, told to us by a supply chain leader for a specialty products company.

> A supply chain product line manager came to work to discover that the plastic containers purchased to hold and ship the company's newest product were insufficient, and some were leaking. This problem would delay thousands of shipments significantly.
>
> The anxious manager called his boss in a panic, blurting out information that was incomplete, irrelevant, and even incorrect. The boss became irritated by this nearly incoherent report, and even though she wasn't getting the details she needed, she began to figure out a solution in her head. Within a couple of minutes, it no longer mattered that the manager was doing a poor job of reporting; his boss was no longer listening.
>
> It took several phone calls and much wasted time to finally clear things up and to devise a plan of action.

When you are balanced, open, and not overthinking, effective communication flows. You have curiosity and goodwill. Communicating is instinctive and responsive. You know when to listen more and when to speak up.

Being balanced not only enables your speaking and listening; it also helps the other person you are communicating with. A calm and clear speaker can help a stressed listener calm down to hear what is being said. A thoughtful listener can help an unbalanced speaker say what he or she really means.

When this synergy happens between people, problems get worked out. You seek first to understand, as the late Stephen Covey wrote in his *Seven*

Habits of Highly Effective People[5], and the other's world makes more sense to you. You see the wisdom in others even when there is disagreement.

Janet is an analyst in a global investment firm. Due to reorganization in her company, she was newly assigned to report to a leader ten years her junior. Janet's new boss began to fill her inbox with suggestions of projects for Janet to work on. In staff meetings, her boss would single Janet out, asking her about the progress on her suggestions. Janet was becoming increasingly defensive, thinking her boss believed she did not know how to do her job.

Janet had been evolving, so she knew that confronting her boss in a defensive state was ill advised. She saw that she was taking the situation personally and that her feelings were coming from her thinking, not the situation. When she felt sufficiently clear and balanced, she met with her boss and simply asked, "Why are you giving me so many projects?" Her boss told Janet that she thought so highly of her that she didn't want her to get bored and move to another part of the company.

After a few good chuckles, Janet and her boss got on the same page and began to work very well together. It was the beginning of an excellent working relationship and a good friendship.

Communication that works is not hard once you understand how it works and what is going on in others' separate realities.

Beyond the Words

A significant portion of communication is nonverbal. When others share their thoughts and experiences with you, they are often sharing layers of thinking, feeling, and meaning behind what they are actually expressing in words. You pick this up through their tone of voice, body language, timing, etc.

Listening to another person beyond their words is not only deeply respectful; it also makes for highly effective communication. It enables you to tune into and grasp more dimensions of what is being communicated—beyond the information someone is sharing.

The curious thing about listening is that it not really something you do. It is something you get out of the way of.

Listening is a natural ability you have that is built into your mental functioning. It is innate radar that can pick up the nonverbal cues and their meaning. Your ego may like to take credit for it, thinking something like, "Aren't I wonderful that I can listen so well and connect to others?" But you're not doing it. It happens when you are in balance and your attention is free to clearly attend to someone.

Listening with this natural, effortless clarity allows for a heartfelt response from inside you. If others sense that you are responding to their feeling and the deeper meaning behind what they are saying, as well as to what they are saying, they tend to feel more deeply understood. They will sense your humanity and appreciate the respect you are affording them.

This kind of listening is at the heart of empathy. It is a core component of what has become known as "emotional intelligence." With empathy, your chances of heartfelt understanding and connection are very good. If you then have something you want to get across, you can frame and phrase it in a way that will work for the other person. You are more likely to be received and understood this way. With empathy, it usually seems more safe and comfortable to discuss any unstated feelings. Doing so can enhance rapport and deepen your human connection with others.

The Really Difficult Conversations

Some conversations seem difficult.

You may have to deliver bad news or challenge someone to step up. You may have to confront an issue that you know is sensitive. In their seminal book, *Difficult Conversations: How to Discuss What Matters Most*, Stone, Patton, & Heen describe three common areas of potential tension in conversations: the facts of a situation, people's feelings, and what the authors termed "identity issues."

Understanding the behind-the-scenes working of the human mind will help you avoid these potential landmines or at least, quickly recover from stepping on one.

For example, knowing the inside→out nature of perception adds a new dimension to the "facts of the situation" if you realize that every person thinks differently and so experiences a unique reality. You will be particularly mindful of this in preparing for a difficult conversation.

Secondly, you will be more awake to the feelings that result when a situation or topic is thought about in a certain way. This awareness allows for a deeper sense of empathy for others as well as an appreciation of your own emotional reaction.

Identity issues are the stickiest of the three. As we stated in Chapter 13, "Getting Over Yourself–Ego Revisited," ego is thinking about yourself that you hold dear. This is the thinking that causes you to feel offended or insulted, or to take what others are doing (or not doing) personally. Feelings of fear, insecurity, anger, and resentment often invade conversations as a result, rendering you and/or the other person unable to participate with balance and maturity. Synergy becomes impossible.

Understanding the power of thought will not make you immune to having identity issues muddy the communication waters, (there's no controlling this power), but it is enormously helpful to be aware of how the system works. You will be increasingly able to catch yourself losing balance, and you will have compassion when that happens to the other person during a conversation.

Whenever both parties in a conversation (or many in a group) reach for mutual understanding and do so in alignment with the design of the way the mind works, they will remain open to insight. Even the stickiest issues can be addressed with respect and care. The outcomes are often transformative.

In Summary:

- The greatest inefficiency in business is the ineffectiveness of communication.
- Effective communication is not only possible, it is enjoyable and easy when you remember that everyone's thinking looks as real to them as yours does to you and you remember that a new perspective is possible at any time.
- When all parties come to a conversation with curiosity and are looking for insight, synergy is likely to happen.
- Empathy occurs within us, when our innate "radar" can hear beyond the words of others, enabling us to register and respond to the nonverbal dimension of communication.
- Difficult conversations go better with awareness of separate realities, where feelings come from, and the stickiness of ego thinking.

twenty

THE ART OF RAPPORT AND RELATIONSHIPS

*Of course when you're a kid, you can be friends with anybody.
Remember when you were a little kid, what were the qualifications?
If someone's in front of my house NOW, that's my friend, they're my
friend. That's it. Are you a grown up? No. Great! Come on in.
Jump up and down on my bed. And if you have anything
in common at all... You like cherry soda?
I like cherry soda! We'll be best friends!*

~ Jerry Seinfeld

This book is filled with stories and examples of rapport and relationships. In fact, our clients have proven that this topic is much simpler than it sometimes looks.

The secret ingredients for rapport and healthy relationships are effective communication (as described in the previous chapter), and an intention to come from a place of balance. When in balance, your respect for the wisdom and insights of others is present.

If you communicate this way and reach a mutual understanding, the innate movement toward rapport and a natural human bond flows. When you are comfortable and relaxed with others, relationships can develop effortlessly and naturally.

What gets in the way of such a natural flow is the outside→in misunderstanding of the mind. Realizing the inside→out paradigm has done a great deal for our relationships in life and for all of our clients.

What is Rapport?

Rapport is a moment-to-moment mutual experience of feeling connected and understood in spite of differences and separate realities. If you have an open, learning conversation with someone long enough to mutually feel understood and connected, rapport will follow. It might take only a few seconds, or it might take much longer.

Rapport doesn't even require words. Eye contact, facial expressions, and body language can communicate understanding and alignment and connection. Sandy had a rich experience of this a few years ago with one of her clients:

I was asked by an executive I was coaching if I would share with his wife some of what he was learning in our sessions. His wife was struggling with anxiety, and he had been unable to be of much help to her. Jessica arrived at my office, and the moment she sat down she started talking rapidly, and she did not stop for nearly twenty minutes. My heart went out to Jessica. I could see she was extremely anxious. I noticed I was feeling empathy for all Jessica seemed to be feeling but was not able to articulate this. I remember thinking that the best thing for me to do was to sit quietly and listen to her as deeply as I could. Finally, Jessica paused, and she was silent for several seconds.

She looked over at me and said, "What are you doing over there?"

"I'm listening," I replied.

She paused again and seemed to settle down. Her rate of speech slowed and she shared with me what was troubling her, much of which she had not shared with anyone, including her husband. Later Jessica remarked that she was very surprised at how safe and comfortable she felt with me, even though she did not know me and I had said very little.

There are, of course, experiences of even deeper rapport. You can have a stable and lasting kind of rapport in which you and another have a history and intention of understanding each other's feelings and perspectives.

Can you have rapport with everyone? We don't advocate that you should, and we would not presume that rapport with everyone is necessary. We are saying that rapport and the feeling of connection is possible with anyone. It is a function of your basic equipment.

Rapport is Key

Have you ever had to get a project done with someone with whom you had no rapport or very little? How well did it go, not having a meeting of minds about what you were doing and why? How efficient was your collaboration? And how pleasant was the experience?

We have all experienced struggles and inefficiencies when rapport was absent.

If all you need to do is create a square peg that fits into someone else's square hole, you don't need much rapport. Most likely, you don't have this kind of job.

Establishing a basic respectful dialogue where mutual understanding and insight creates synergy will help, no matter what you have to accomplish with another person. When an entire team experiences this kind of rapport and relationship, the team has the prerequisite foundation for high performance, no matter the challenges.

Getting into rapport with people you work with does not mean you necessarily have to like them. However, we are saying that rapport will give you an incomparable advantage in all your interactions.

Getting Past Unconscious Bias

It is very common to have judgments, attitudes, and prejudices about people. We would be hard pressed to find a person alive who loves everyone on the planet. You are bombarded by others' thoughts and attitudes about people, and it is hard to avoid those opinions. In an organization, you pass around impressions and judgments about others that become the realities about those people. No one we know is immune to this phenomenon.

These prejudices operate in the background and are hard to see. Keeping your balance in the face of others' biases, and remaining aware of your own, will enhance your ability to get along with those who are challenging for you. Awareness of the invisible power of thought and seeing the outside→in misunderstanding that most people live in are both enormously helpful.

We have noticed an interesting phenomenon when we share insight principles with individuals and groups. As our clients wake up to the invisible power of thought and find a home base of good feeling, they begin to gravitate to more curiosity and openness as a way of being. They begin to see the thinking that takes them away from that way of being and let go of it more often and more easily.

Prejudices fall squarely into the category of thoughts that interfere with openness and goodwill toward others.

Being confronted with others' biases is difficult for most people and can easily trigger strong reactions. If you can draw on your understanding of how minds work and remain open and curious, it is easier to see how others innocently misunderstand the nature of thought and perception. You see others' prejudices and egos in action and don't react to them. You find the possibility of having kinder, more compassionate feelings and become more capable of establishing rapport with people who, on the surface, you don't feel deserve the effort. You even find you can do it easily at times.

Joe was the CEO of a major subsidiary of a global conglomerate. Unfortunately for Joe, his corporate contact, Harry (to whom he effectively reported), was not one of his favorite people. Joe's habit was to not suffer fools gladly. Unfortunately, in his eyes, Harry was not competent enough to be his boss.

You can imagine how most of their interactions went.

Joe's learning of insight principles had given him helpful insights about the workings of his own mind, but when it came to Harry, there was little change. We would be coaching Joe on his meetings with Harry, and he would rant and rave about his boss. "Yes, I know it's all thought," Joe said, "but Harry is still an idiot!"

Over time, Joe realized how his and Harry's minds operated. Our coaching about the art of rapport began to sink in. He became less interested in his reactions and attitudes about Harry and more curious about how to make the relationship work.

On one of our regular coaching calls, Joe shared a recent interesting conversation with Harry. "You know how I always have that knee-jerk reaction when I get on the phone with Harry?" Joe started. "Well this time it was not so bad. I was able to get out from under that thinking pretty quickly. The next thing that happened was quite amazing and a bit surreal."

He went on, "This time Harry was on me for a budget cut in marketing. I was settled, and maybe because of that, it occurred to me to ask him why. He replied, 'So we could improve the profit potential of the business.' I asked him, 'If it's about profit, why cut marketing spending?' He replied, 'The less we spend on marketing, the more profits we make.'

"In that moment, I realized that Harry had completely different expertise and experience from me, and actually did not understand my business at all. Since he was not from the business-to-customer world, he did not know that when you create a new product, you have to advertise it so people know it exists, i.e., if you cut marketing, you hurt profit. It occurred to me that maybe Harry wasn't an idiot, just ill prepared for his role. When I explained what Harry did not know, it seemed to make sense, and he agreed that we should not cut marketing.

"And then the surreal thing happened." Joe continued. "As we ended the call, Harry commented that this conversation with me had been the most pleasant he could remember."

> "We're still not the best of friends, and we are not going on holiday together any time soon, but we have a new level of rapport. Harry seems more open with me; he listens and mostly agrees now. It feels like he's on my side. Finally!"
>
> Joe learned that he could be in rapport with anyone.

Rapport is the currency for being effective with others in business.

Rapport is not about being best friends with everyone. It is about having a sense of who a person is and where they are coming from, and interacting with them with those elements in mind. With this essential information you will see how best to proceed given what you are trying to accomplish. You will also find out how deep your partnership can go to get things done and collaborate even more going forward.

Overcoming Silos

An entire team can have rapport. We have already described the synergy that results, such as in Chapter 18, when John and his team developed the rapport to discuss their differences about a new joint venture.

There can also be strong rapport between teams and throughout an entire organization. The potential for synergy, innovation, and productivity is endless when this happens. We have shared a number of examples of team synergy in this book so far and devote a whole chapter to this later on (see Chapter 22, Team Synergy). History and industry are full of fabulous examples. The collaboration among Reagan, Gorbachev, and Thatcher over a number of years that eventually led to the fall of the Berlin wall was a great example of rapport making a real difference.

Conversely, there have been countless failures that can be attributed to a lack of rapport. In the early 2000s, when Sony was desperate to recapture it's prominence in digital music media, the inability to maintain rapport between its music division, software developers, and its programmers led to the very prominent failure of Sony Connect. Sony never recaptured the digital music title from Apple.

When there is a lack of rapport between teams or parts of an organization, many describe this as being stuck in silos. (Farm silos house different grains or crops and stand alone, not connected to one another). It is amazing how many times we have encountered teams within the same company that were working in competitive or antagonistic ways, undermining or interfering with what each other were trying to accomplish.

Regardless of how much acrimony and prejudice we encounter in these situations, when we help them see the inside→out power of their own thoughts and insights, they come to see the folly of their thinking and find common ground to start over with a new vision, spirit, and energy.

Here's an example.

We were asked to help two research and development teams sort out their differences. The two teams worked sequentially in the product development process (i.e., the first team completed work that it then handed off to the second). The company was in a fast-paced and increasingly competitive field; streamlined, agile performance was critical to maintaining their market share.

When we met the two teams, although there was no out-right warfare, the two leaders did not get along well, and, not surprisingly, neither did their people. Disagreements, poor hand-offs, missed deadlines, blame, and general unease were daily occurrences.

Even though it meant a larger than usual class, we met with the two teams and their leaders in the same session. Tensions settled considerably as they collectively learned about the inside→out nature of experience, their built-in design for success, and the innate qualities of the mind.

One implication that became newly obvious to them was separate realities (see Chapter 10). They could see that other people weren't bad or ill intentioned; they were seeing different worlds and didn't realize it.

As observers, we could see the entire group become more open and reflective as they relaxed and began enjoying each other. In very short order they concluded that their teams were not on the same page about timelines or targets. More importantly, they collectively realized that a shared vision was imperative. It took the group fifty minutes of focused discussion and effective listening to come up with a vision and a plan on how to move forward. They even came up with a new name for their combined work and a logo to match. They were having more fun than they thought they could have together.

By the end of our time with them, the group reinvented the way the industry did their two process steps and halved the lead time!

> As you can imagine, with a clear imperative and good rapport, implementation followed easily. The quality of shared thinking continues to improve, as do the relationships between the teams.

And as with individuals, rapport between teams is an ongoing endeavor, only with more moving parts!

Advanced Rapport: Influencing Without Authority

An important challenge leaders face is having accountability for a result but no authority to pull it off. It can take concerted effort to persuade other leaders with different agendas and responsibilities to devote their time, resources, and energy to help you. Without air cover (someone higher up in the organization with the authority to support your efforts), you have to rely on rapport to influence others to help you out.

The rapport that you need can often be overlooked.

It is easy to assume that a simple explanation of your needs will incite others to come to the aid of your projects with goodwill and understanding. After all, you all want the company to be successful. Shouldn't others take your project needs seriously? And indeed, the other leaders may understand and even empathize with your challenge but simply lack the bandwidth to help you. Then there are other leaders who, with the best of intentions, agree to help but don't follow through in the ways that you expected.

Why do these things happen so often?

They happen because we underestimate the need for, and the power of, mutual understanding and connection. We don't take the time to create the rapport that will inspire others to help.

An interesting example of this happened to a client of ours, Donald, who was asked to develop and then drive a company-wide profitability improvement initiative.

Donald had spent most of his career at other companies in key lead positions. He had recently come to this company and was temporarily asked to head up a company-wide initiative where he had to interact with peers rather than having a team of direct reports to execute a large agenda. He had a commanding style and was not used to having to establish rapport before asking for big things from others. He described his challenge to us and how it resolved itself while he was learning about rapport in new ways:

"The case for change was obvious. We had an earnings gap and had to improve our profitability across all our businesses. Given the highly process-bound culture we had, I devised a plan, wrote it up, and sent it out to the division and functional leaders. I was very surprised when not much happened. When I started to meet with each key leader to reiterate my initial communication, I noticed the feeling was not all that warm and fuzzy. Polite and cordial, but nothing more than that."

As we discussed this challenge with Donald, we were curious to find out what he knew about separate realities. Having worked with thousands of people and scores of direct reports in his career, he claimed to always be interested in other people and how to support them.

"I have gotten on well with just about everyone," he claimed, and from what we had heard, it was true.

We talked at length about the power of thought to create people's realities from within and how much we underestimate how different our realities are. We also discussed the rapport that is required when asking very busy people to add more to their plates.

At one point in the discussion, Donald blurted out, "The plan makes sense to me, but I have no idea whether it makes sense to the sixteen people I need to work with on this project. Maybe they don't see it my way."

Then Donald had another insight. "I really need to connect with these folks to get my vision across. I need to get them on board. These are smart people. It probably feels awkward having someone from 'Corporate' show up to tell them how to do their jobs." Although the profitability initiative had clear merit, unless the leaders could see it for themselves, all Donald would get was resistance.

Later, Donald told us, "I saw that I needed to make a shift in my next one-on-one meeting. It occurred to me to spend time connecting and listening to what was on the guy's plate before discussing my project. I then brought up the initiative but started with an apology for dropping this in on him from nowhere.

"Once the feeling was good between us, the apology was warmly accepted, the merits of the program were openly discussed, and good suggestions were made about

> how to move things forwards productively. Since I had
> my insight and changed my approach, things have been
> moving ahead very well."

The kind of deep listening and understanding Donald shifted to got his peers' attention and generated heartfelt rapport. For Donald, understanding their realities deeply enough helped him see how his request for help fit into their worlds. It is easy to make a plea for help. It is another thing to learn enough about the ins and outs of another's needs to know how to frame your request with respect and consideration. This is a crucial component of influencing without authority.

An interesting phenomenon we often see is that people make the effort to understand you depending on the depth to which they feel understood. When you have too many assumptions and are too busy to really understand others, influencing without authority is a difficult, if not impossible, proposition.

> **It is easy to forget that your reality may
> not be part of another person's reality.**

Sustainable, Healthy Relationships

Though we have known about insight principles collectively for more than sixty years, we still get in bad moods. We get grumpy, busy minded, or caught up in our insecurities, and when this happens, we can lose rapport and our relationships can suffer. Thought is powerful enough to create a reality with strong feelings that are not balanced or wise. Even in close relationships that are usually harmonious, you can be distracted or reactive and fail to experience understanding and connection.

This is the human condition.

So what makes for a successful, healthy, and enduring relationship over time?

We cannot overstate how much our understanding of insight principles has meant to our relationships. When you realize, in the moment, that your feelings are coming only from your own thoughts, you simply stop blaming others for them. Relationships are no longer a place to point fingers or to get what you think you need to be happy.

**When you are aligned with how the mind is designed
to work, you understand that wisdom, insight,
and effective communication are always possible.**

Writing this book together has been, at times, challenging, wonderful, insightful, revelatory, thrilling, annoying, and much more. Overall, though, it has been a great learning experience and has deepened our understanding of insight principles, of each other, and the rapport we have with each other. This is true even after working closely together for many years.

When we felt stuck, we didn't grind away. We knew that our creativity would flow again when we were fresh. We learned to trust that our synergy would return and when it did, the productivity would be exponentially better, with more wisdom and perspective. This knowledge made discovering things together lots of fun and our own learning a joy.

There were times when we got upset with our process or with each other. When we saw the role our own thinking was playing, we'd take responsibility for it. We were able to remain patient and trust that things would eventually right themselves, and we would have an insight, learn from our differences, and observe the wisdom in each other.

When we reacted with upset feelings, we were able to look inside to see that it was our own thinking getting in our way. This was difficult for each of us at different points, as a direction or strategy for the writing or the design of the book seemed really important to one or another of us. Sometimes our egos got the best of us.

Taking responsibility for our own ego thinking and reactions was both hard and humbling. It was also enormously freeing to finally come to see that it was just a bunch of thoughts we had been holding onto. Having experienced the stickiness of ego for ourselves, it was easier for us to be patient and compassionate with each other. (Fortunately, all three of us didn't have reactions at the same time!)

In the end, we have come through the process evolved from where we started, more deeply appreciative of the wisdom and essence of each other, and grateful for having been on a productive and growth-filled journey together. With good understanding, it can be this way for you in any of your relationships.

> **Over time, a commitment to rapport and good feeling engenders trust, warmth, and a joy of working or being in life together.**

Seeing Others with New Eyes

Your thinking changes and evolves all the time. You can't help it. The same is true for everyone else. Hence, everyone's reality is always changing and evolving. Life is energy in motion, and that motion never stops. Whenever you encounter someone you know well, it is easy to make a lot of assumptions about the other person. But they have changed since you last saw them—sometimes a little, sometimes a lot.

If you are married or in a partnership of any kind, it might seem that you have been partnered with the same person over time. But that is just your thinking. If you look closely, you'll realize you have been partnering with lots of different versions of the person, and a new version is always showing up. This is what can make relationships rich, interesting, and rewarding.

It also makes relationships great opportunities for learning and growth. We consistently observed this as we wrote this book. Just when we thought we had each other figured out, one of us would write something surprising or offer up a completely new view about a point or chapter. It was often challenging, but more often a delightful surprise to experience greater clarity and understanding as we learned from each other.

Whenever we have fresh thinking, our partnership evolves. The freshness is always in the eye of the beholder.

In Summary:

- Rapport is a moment-to-moment mutual experience of feeling connected and understood in spite of differences and separate realities.
- Healthy relationships are sustainable when people are oriented toward the feelings that come with balance, wisdom, and insight.
- Seeing your ego thinking for what it is, and being able to get out from under it, are powerful abilities that facilitate successful relationships with others.
- Relationships remain rich and rewarding when you understand that new versions of yourself and others are always showing up.

twenty one

THOSE "DIFFICULT" PEOPLE

What you see is what you get!

~ Flip Wilson

You likely have at least one difficult person in your life. This is the person you find challenging to connect with or to influence. You may have reasons for your struggle: your personalities clash, you have different values, you are too competitive with each other, etc. And yet you may have a productive relationship with someone else who is very much like your difficult person.

You may also have the experience of having a difficult person transform into an easy-to-relate-to-person. What happened? Who changed?

Rethinking Difficult

It's easy to forget how powerful thought is. You live in the experience of your moment-to-moment thinking. When you think about someone as being difficult, you see that person as difficult, and the strategies that come to mind for interacting with that person will be limited to strategies you would use with a difficult person. When a person looks innocent, misguided, or insecure to you, whatever interaction comes to your mind will be in service of this perception. If you see a person as capable of wisdom and insight but as lost in thought without realizing it, you will act accordingly.

When you forget how powerful thought is, you forget that the experience of "difficult" comes from you.

Here's a common, nonwork example. When children are tired, they are often cranky and uncooperative. Many a cranky child has uttered the phrase, "Daddy (or Mommy), I hate you!" For most parents, this outburst is ignored and the tired child is guided to bed as soon as possible. The child is seen as tired, not evil, and the disrespectful behavior is seen as something a tired child does.

On the other hand, there have been times when the tired, cranky child actually looks evil! When you are off balance, your perspective changes. You temporarily lose your ability to see innocence or to have compassion. The flow of insights to guide you through interactions gets blocked, like water in a kinked garden hose.

This is Not Positive Thinking

We are not suggesting that you should make yourself see people in a positive light. First of all, this would take effort, and you already have enough to do. Second, it rarely works when you need it the most.

Thoughts come into your mind at the speed of light. In the blink of an eye, you find yourself deeply embedded in a view about someone and in a reaction about the behavior you are witnessing. What now? As we have stated throughout the book, understanding how powerful thought is does not preclude you from biases or reactions. Knowing about gravity does not keep you from falling. Your understanding can, however, wake you up to what is happening within your mind and allow you to take another look. And then another. And then another.

Here's a story told to us by a participant in one of our programs.

Tom is an experienced manager of people. He described his current team of twenty skilled assemblers working in the commercial trucking industry as one of the best teams he has ever managed. The majority of his group functioned independently and well with just Tom's encouragement and occasional assistance.

Then there was Charlie. As Tom told the class about Charlie, we could see the frustration on his face and hear it in his voice. Tom had met his match in Charlie. Charlie is a thirty-something-year-old assembler who had been with the company for five years. Tom, surprisingly, was his fourth manager, even though the company rarely moved assemblers around due to the technical nature of the job and the time it took to become proficient.

Tom described Charlie as very difficult. Charlie was often tardy, his work quality was inconsistent, and his work output was well below that of the other assemblers, though sometimes he excelled. Tom had many discussions with Charlie, and Charlie always had a good explanation for why his performance wasn't up to par. "You wouldn't believe the creative excuses this guy could come up with."

"Charlie is a difficult employee," Tom told us in class. "He takes more of my time than the rest of the team for far less return. I'm not making this up in my head. This is not just my thinking."

Tom liked the insight principles program, but by the time it concluded he had not reported any insights about "difficult" Charlie. Two weeks later, during our customary follow-up call, things had changed. Riding in his car the first day back to work after the class, Tom was enjoying the countryside he drove through on his way to work. The thought of Charlie crossed his mind and, to Tom's surprise, it brought a smile to his face. "I couldn't believe it. I was thinking about Charlie **and** smiling! But, you know, he looked different to me. He looked a bit like one of my teenage sons instead of the thirty-plus-year-old man that he is. I started thinking about how I would handle Charlie if he was my son, and some insight came."

"So I met with Charlie that morning and told him that I had lost confidence in him. I explained what happens when a team loses confidence in one of its members. Then I spelled out why this was now his problem and not mine. I told him to come up with a plan to get my confidence back."

Tom shared all this with Charlie without his usual frustration. "I was matter-of-fact, but this time I had some hopefulness. I felt like Charlie was actually capable of rising to his potential." After that conversation, Charlie started improving. It was still early in the process, but Tom's relationship with Charlie was different.

More importantly, Tom experienced the power of his thinking as the source of his personal reality. He saw that his limited thinking about Charlie as a difficult person kept him locked in strategies that were ineffective. Once that thinking changed, new strategies came to mind.

As we quoted the late comic Flip Wilson at the start of this chapter, this is the only way the mind works.

Some People Seem Just Impossible!

You do not get out of bed in the morning and wonder how you will or should behave on any given day. You simply wake up and thought begins to flow. You experience your thinking. For the most part, you do not choose your reality. Neither does anyone else. And without realizing it, your ego runs your world according to your desires, fears, and attitudes.

When you realize this deeply enough, you know that other people's realities are their world as well. It is their life. You might not agree with them or find them easy to communicate with, but you can respect the phenomenon that creates their world.

If others appear to interfere with your productivity or disadvantage you, it is easy to react and lose your balance. It is common to become angry or defensive if someone consistently interferes with your efforts or desires or threatens your well-being. However, there are many people who don't get angry or defensive and stay cool in the face of those people. They don't let their thinking and reactions get the best of them.

Regardless of how strong your reactions are to someone else's behavior, the feelings are coming from your mind. It won't help to react in most instances. Your balance and insight are needed to get the best from yourself in these kinds of situations. To us, these situations are always an opportunity to see the invisible power of thought within more deeply, in service of staying cool to create a desirable outcome.

Ken's son, Zander, had a challenging period in middle school with a few other young men who were older and bigger and enjoyed teasing and bullying. When Zander was the target of their mistreatment, he took it personally and got very upset. His mood was grumpy, and his participation at home and at school suffered. This went on for some time before Ken and his wife, Kailia, found out what was happening.

When Zander finally let them know, Ken and Kailia spoke to the teachers at school, who attended to the situation, and the bullying stopped. Some of the teasing continued in a subtler way, however, and it was still disturbing to Zander. Ken and Kailia could see that that intervening at school was only a partial solution, since teasing and bullying could happen again in other places. The family was able to use the event to talk about thought, feelings, and the inside→out paradigm.

It took a number of discussions, but Zander's confidence and clarity grew with each conversation. He truly came to see that his feelings and reactions were between him and his own mind. He also realized that his reactions fueled the teasing kids' behaviors.

Whenever he remembered his insights, he kept his balance. He didn't remember every time, but it got better.

The family had to keep reinforcing this understanding with Zander over a number of weeks. Eventually, Ken and his wife didn't hear about these incidents anymore. At one point they asked Zander how things were going with those boys. "Fine," he replied.

"What do you mean?" they had to ask.

"After learning to ignore them, I could see they were being stupid. They are just into bothering people for sport. Instead of feeling bad about them, I feel bad for them. They are just being jerks."

"What about your bad feelings?" they asked.

"I stopped having them. Kids like that can't make me feel bad," he said.

No matter how troubling others' behaviors can be, you can become curious and see their innocence. By innocence, we do not mean you see everyone's behavior or intentions as acceptable, appropriate, or desirable. We mean that you will see that people experience what they think is real without realizing that it is their thinking. If you were having the same thinking as the other person, you would be having the same experience and likely acting in the same way. "There by the grace of God go I," as they say.

As mentioned earlier, we have seen this realization move people off their reactions in prison, courtrooms, and the most challenging situations you will find in any business.

When we first met Jeremy, he was a lead scientist in his division at an electronics research firm. Four times a year, he met with seven of his counterparts to make long-term strategic choices about technology. Unfortunately, these meetings were mostly a waste of time. One of his peers, Bill, always came in with a set view and was not open to changing his mind. As a result, the meetings were full of arguments and bad feelings. Not much got accomplished.

"Bill is impossible. No one can work with him—but we have to," Jeremy told us. "I can't stand the guy. We get eight very senior and busy people to meet four times a year for three hours and get little done, all because of Bill."

During his individual leadership retreat with us, Jeremy's frustration began to turn to curiosity as the power of thought and the implication of separate realities began to sink in for him. He eventually left us relaxed and cautiously hopeful about how things might turn out relative to Bill.

The next time we spoke, Jeremy reported interesting developments. He had met with Bill and asked him directly about the team meetings. Jeremy remembers that he was neither annoyed nor on edge, as was typical for him in Bill's presence. Rather, he was curious about why a very smart person would be doing something so strange.

What he learned surprised him.

"When I spoke to Bill, he readily admitted to his unbendable stance. He explained how he would get confused in meetings with multiple people. When he was a young scientist, he decided that, prior to any important discussion, he would sit quietly, formulate his opinion, and come up with all the arguments to support his view.

"As soon as Bill explained himself, I saw that he is not trying to be troublesome or difficult. He had developed a coping strategy, which worked for him, but for no one else." Jeremy saw that, in his own way, Bill's wisdom had provided him with a partial answer for preventing confusion in meetings. It made perfect sense.

When Jeremy asked Bill if he had noticed the impact of his style, all he got was a blank look—he clearly had never considered the effect of his coping strategy on others! This was another piece of information for Jeremy. Bill did not notice what was happening around him.

Now Jeremy had a better grasp of the situation. Without respect for Bill's world, he would not have asked Bill questions in the manner that he did. And without the neutral, curious delivery, how might Bill have taken those questions?

It's Not Personal!

If you could see inside the mind of a so-called difficult person, you would find a great deal of thinking they are reacting to. People who are perceived as difficult often feel threatened and believe they have to protect themselves. How do we know this? We have been difficult people from time to time, and our understanding of human functioning has allowed us to look within, to the source of our experience.

We have also noticed that when we have been unsuccessful at addressing a difficult person as a leader, a team member, friend, or family member, much of our frustration came from the same thinking we described above. We became defensive and got pulled off balance. We took the situation personally or went on the offensive. This is a very ordinary, human thing to do.

The only antidote that we have found for these ineffective interactions is our understanding of how the mind works. Here's how that understanding helped a deteriorating work relationship get back on track.

Nick was Jonathan's difficult person, and Jonathan was Nick's. When Nick began reporting to Jonathan, their team's momentum and productivity took a nosedive. When Jonathan spoke, Nick heard a tone in his voice that he described as "superior" or "the expert." Once Nick heard this tone, he stopped listening to Jonathan. He missed pertinent facts that Jonathan would then have to repeat. Jonathan would get irritated, seeing Nick as disrespectful and rude. Their interactions deteriorated from there.

Nick attended one of our insight programs and woke up to the inside→out nature of his feelings. He shared a conversation he and Jonathan had soon after the program.

"Jonathan kept repeating things, as if I was stupid, and I stopped listening. We went around and around for a while and eventually ended the meeting without getting much accomplished. I went back to my office with my usual feeling of being talked down to by Jonathan. But when I looked at my own thinking instead of what Jonathan said, I saw my part in it. I always had a defensive attitude and feeling about him. Once in my defensive

> reaction, which I blamed on Jonathan, I couldn't listen. This put Jonathan off. When I saw this, I got my bearings, and I returned to Jonathan's office and apologized."
>
> "I told Jonathan that we should have bailed on the conversation as soon as we stopped listening. Jonathan agreed with me. Then he asked me what I had heard him say. I shared what I had heard, and he listened. We soon worked the issue out. It was, by far, the smoothest interaction we have ever had."

Nick remembered that his feelings were coming from inside, not from the situation with Jonathan, and he calmed down. Nick also had developed more faith that rapport could flow easily with anyone, and he decided to take responsibility to find opportunities for rapport.

When you remember that you feel your thinking, this alerts you to what is going on inside both you and others. Ultimately, you cannot change another person, but you can help to create an environment that brings out the best in others. With inner balance, your common sense and clarity can usually move things forward.

In Summary:

- If you think you are dealing with a difficult person, everything you say and everything you do will make it worse.
- With wisdom and insight, your view of challenging people can evolve, affording you better options for effective interactions.
- Insight about where your inner reactions to others truly come from will enable you to stay balanced and at home in yourself, regardless of the person with whom you have to interact.

twenty two

TEAM SYNERGY

"And you know, two heads are better than one."

~ Joni Mitchell

As we pointed out earlier in the book, synergy has a certain kind of feeling. That feeling arises when people's minds are open and when there is respect for the capacity for insight within everyone involved. Ego thinking takes a back seat to the flow of insight, both individually and collectively. This feeling can be rich and deep. Cohesion emerges in the group. Alignment happens easily. Breakthrough ideas become ordinary and possibilities flourish.

Teams that have been together for a long time or that have worked together successfully on a stretch goal may naturally fall into this synergy. For many other teams, finding synergy is hit-and-miss. Egos can flare, disagreement can stymy listening, and engagement can fluctuate, especially when the topic of discussion is controversial.

Learning how the mind works can smooth out these kinks. As we explained in Chapter 17 on Connection and Synergy, it is natural to move toward alignment and collective wisdom when minds are open and respectful. Almost any group that is willing can learn to allow natural synergy to happen.

Understanding how the mind works is a valuable component to make that reliable.

We were asked to help a $5 billion-revenue biotech company address an earnings shortfall. Their plan for $600 million in EBIT had been rejected; their holding company was requesting $700 million. They were a smart and resourceful organization that had achieved breakthrough results many times before, but this time they were stumped. Upon hearing of the directive, they had taken a senior group off-site and "sweated" the problem for three days, but that had only yielded $35 million of ideas. It was now five weeks from the start of that earnings cycle, and, to make matters worse, the market was softening to the point that even $600 million looked unlikely.

At the CEO's request, a team of their top twenty-five people went through our Insight Synergy Program, with the explicit goal of uncovering ways to bridge the looming earnings gap. Although the program had been hastily organized, the group was very mature and experienced—none with fewer than twenty-five years of service—and, correspondingly, had a fabulous collection of industry and company knowledge.

As we started to share the inside→out nature of life and the participants' minds began to settle, we observed a wonderful phenomenon in the room. Although no one said it outright, there was a deep feeling of love and connection.

Collectively, they had been through a lot together, personally and professionally, and as the excess thinking dropped away, what was left was a feeling of deep mutual respect and caring.

We pointed out that these caring, loving feelings were natural and flowed effortlessly when their minds were not caught up or stressed. The team resonated with us because they had experienced this space many times before. They quickly made the connection between their mutual openness and a reliable flow of new ideas. They instinctively saw that without mental constraints or fear, they could explore anything and be brilliant

Shortly after their realization, we moved into the problem-resolution phase of our program. Buoyed by their strong feeling of connection, the participants were able to listen to each other without the filters common in highly experienced people. As they learned to stay oriented to this feeling, every idea or question was viewed as interesting and worthy of reflection.

They worked in functional and cross-functional groups, and essentially sat around reflecting on what seemed novel or curious. For example, someone asked members of the sales team why they always exceeded their forecasts. What came out was a general concern about year-end bonuses resulting in many people artificially lowering their targets, which, of course, they then exceeded. This caused operations to scramble at the year's end, with unplanned production costs and the loss of considerable profits. A cascade of fascinating ideas followed about how to change sales incentives and upgrade the product mix.

Likewise, the General Counsel asked about the length of their licensing agreements, typically twenty-five years. Couldn't they be shortened and some of the money asked for up front?

The ideas ranged from the reinforcement of what was already known, to revisiting previously discarded ideas, and then to completely new, unimagined ideas. The list was long and rich, and everyone seemed to be having fun.

Within a day and a half, they had collectively identified EBIT improvement ideas totaling over $400 million! This list was triaged into about $200 million of discrete projects that, when implemented, allowed the company to get very close to its earnings target that year.

Understanding how the mind works, and that it is only your thinking in the way of your creative capacity for out-of-the box insight, enables teams to have synergy in the face of problems big and small. Every situation is an opportunity to engage with clarity and perspective and with the confidence that wise, productive thinking is always within reach.

Crises or seemingly impossible tasks may appear to be the catalyst to bring out the best in teams. But as we see it, when people understand their mental life and focus on what needs to get done, insights and new perspectives begin to flow.

Solving Intractable Problems

We have countless examples of business teams and individuals who solved critical or intractable problems once they understood how the mind works. Here is an example.

A number of years ago, we were asked to help a specialty products company address a critical business issue. They had tried just about everything to solve it, and things were getting worse. They were desperate.

Basically, the company's previously sound but aggressive Asia Strategy wasn't working. Despite the company's having forced the fragmented and disruptive local producers out of business and building their own state-of-the-art facility, those same local producers had reappeared with new plants that were financed without much regard for normal Western economics. Our client's competition had just gotten tougher.

They tried to counter this by tying up the demand and forming a joint venture with the largest regional consumer. Within a year, this new partner had struck an equivalent deal with the company's main global rival.

Despite multiple corrective initiatives, it was clear that continuing to think about the dilemma the same way was not going to fix it. And time was running out.

We were asked to help the global multifunctional team responsible for solving the problem.

Going into the session, the pervasive belief among the team was that solving the problem in the four days set aside for our program was unrealistic. However, after a short exposure to insight principles, the team surfaced a series of insights that completely reframed the strategic issue, suggested a solution, and pointed to a previously-hidden fatal flaw in 40 percent of the firm's base business. The team called the solution "the three miracles."

Not to leave you in suspense, the team socialized the solution, gained support, and the three miracles were implemented via a Design-For-Six-Sigma project. The impact was estimated to be a $40 million annual profit improvement in their base business.

A year later, the solution and savings were being realized. When asked about the impact, the CEO explained, "We went from having sixty of our top executives constantly worrying about the problem to a team of ten people successfully solving it."

Let us say more about this example.

How Did it Happen?

If you had been a fly on the wall during the four days with the team, you would have observed them coming to understand the nature of thought and the inherent design of the mind. Once those insights occurred:

1. The team settled down. They paused often as they were listening or sharing ideas. The feeling in the room became relaxed and peaceful. The personal mental noise in each of them quieted down, and they could hear each other and their own new thinking more easily.

2. The collective back-of-the-mind assumptions also diminished. Their fixed, collective way of thinking about the problem dis-

solved. New thoughts emerged, sometimes as an answer, more often as a question. They were able to get past the usual spoken and often unspoken thoughts, such as:

"Well that won't work."

"Who are you to have that opinion?"

"This is how it has always worked."

3. The team got curious about the problem and started to discuss the issues with each other in a very different way. They developed more respect for their separate realities and realized everyone has a unique way of seeing things. They began to look for the wisdom in each person's perspective. If someone had a different opinion, for example, it didn't make sense to automatically assume he or she was wrong. They began to wonder what others were seeing. You could sense a hopefulness that something productive was going to happen.

On the morning of the third day of their meeting, a massive insight popped up. The room went silent, and everyone just sat there taking in the new idea.

A few people did get a bit insecure.

"It can't be that simple."

"They'll laugh at us when we report back to the Executive Committee!"

"There has to be a flaw in this solution."

But, fortunately, enough of the team was in balance, so they heard the concerns and had some really thoughtful responses. The main response was to spend the rest of their time together (1.5 days) trying to shoot holes in the new solution.

The more they poked, discussed, and stayed curious, the better the solution looked; in fact, it was during this stage of the meeting that another massive insight hit—there was a previously unseen fatal flaw in 40 percent of their base business. Fortunately, their solution would also start to address this flaw, adding more value and credibility to the solution.

The meeting ended with the solution intact. As the team headed off to share the solution with the key stakeholders and functions that had to implement it, they remained curious. After all, who knows what else they might see?

Warning!

It is probably worth adding a slight note of caution. It is possible to read the above description of what happened and create a process or a set of things to do. That won't work, and it is definitely not what the team did. The secret to the success of the meeting was not the process. The horsepower came from what the team learned about the human mind.

Their own understanding of insight principles enabled them to notice and question their thinking and soften their own positions. They knew to attend to the feeling in themselves and in the room. Being balanced and feeling at home inside themselves and with each other, they instinctively knew what to say, what to ask, how to frame the conversation, when to pause, etc. The understanding held the power, not the process.

Synergistic Meetings

A colleague of ours once quipped, after attending a business client's meeting, that if he was told that he had one month to live, he would want to spend his remaining time in their meetings—because it would feel like an eternity!

Imagine what it would be like if your meetings were places of deep listening, quiet reflection, innovative thinking, and collaborative planning. This is not a pipedream; it can become the norm for you.

When teams see how thought, feelings, and insight, work from the inside→out, the feeling of a conversation becomes the barometer for whether the team is heading toward synergy or not. Team synergy then begins to be the norm from meeting to meeting. Teams become hopeful that synergy will happen whenever they are together. This is a fabulous way to do teamwork and get a lot done. People who experience this synergy just love to come to work.

In Summary:

- Realizing the resources of the human mind can enable a team to consistently generate innovation and breakthrough business results.
- Processes and techniques cannot reliably produce team synergy the way the mind is naturally designed to do.
- The joy and productivity of working in synergy can become a new normal for any team.

twenty three

INNATE LEADERSHIP

A leader is best when people barely know he exists,
when his work is done, his aim fulfilled,
they will say: we did it ourselves.

~ Lao Tzu

Everything we have learned and observed about the powerful and invisible principles working behind the scenes in all people has led us to conclude that anyone can lead.

Clearly, only a small set of people may be suited to lead a financial services organization, a hospital, or a football team. There are essential elements to leadership, such as knowledge, aptitude, and experience. But we are pointing in a different direction.

There is an inner dimension of leadership that exists in everyone, whether it ever rises to the surface or not.

The Inner Dimension of Leadership

Understanding the inside→out nature of experience changes the way you look at leadership.

Leadership is an innate characteristic built into your design for success. Clarity and confidence are at its core. When you are balanced and feeling at home in yourself, it is easy to see with perspective, and your insights move you to respond intelligently in ways that are productive for you and others.

Here's an example of how anyone can rise to leadership when they understand more about how their mind works:

A technology company with $1.2 billion in revenues asked for our help. The CFO was caught cooking the books and the beloved founder and CEO of twenty-five years was forced to resign, as were all but two of the top sixteen leaders in the company. A new CEO brought in a new leadership team from his previous company, along with a very different culture.

Many changes made by the new leadership were extremely unpopular. The workforce was in revolt. Productivity was down, as were morale and revenues. More time was spent complaining and blaming at the water coolers than getting work done.

The company hired us to help. After sharing what we know with some of the key leaders, it was decided to run an insight principles program, first with the leadership and then with nine hundred engineers. David was in one of the first programs. He was an engineer in his twenties who had been hired just prior to the leadership shakeup. He was angry and vocal about his frustration and disappointment. He couldn't relax, and he didn't let up for the first day and a half of our program.

Toward the end of the second day, he began to have some insights. He began to see that he was not a victim of the situation, even though the situation wasn't what he had signed up for when he came to the company. Then he noticed that there were some people in the organization who were not fazed by the changes. When David came to understand the role of his mind in his perceived victimization, he relaxed. Once that happened, his own situation looked completely different to him.

In addition, a frequent complaint among the workforce was that Bill, the new CEO, was disrespectful. The tone and language of his speeches and emails lacked respect for the culture everyone had grown to love. David, and many others, had felt insulted and bothered by these communications. With his new insight, it occurred to David that Bill was probably doing the best he could to lead a company whose culture he did not understand. Maybe he didn't realize the impact of his approach.

David decided to do something.

At the conclusion of the afternoon session, David headed up to the C suite and asked to see Bill. With confidence and warmth, David asked Bill if he would like to hear some reactions people were having to his emails. Bill was at first a bit put off. It was highly unusual for someone at David's level to come in and give him feedback like this. In addition, there was considerable tension in the company between the culture of the new leaders and that of the legacy company.

David explained the program he was attending. "I told Bill that I saw something that might be very helpful. I respectfully explained that, since it seemed so critical, I thought it best not to go through too many channels to get this information to him."

Bill saw David's goodwill and wholesome intent, and he relaxed. David told Bill that his emails had language and a perceived tone that people were finding offensive, given the culture the company had enjoyed for many years. Then he suggested other ways to word his messages. Bill was grateful for the help, and his approach and language changed that afternoon.

David's innate capacity for leadership arose when he saw his reactions for what they were and his mind cleared. He saw what could be done, got inspired to act, and was undaunted. It looked to him like common sense. It was obvious that someone had to let Bill know what was going on.

Courage?

Did David decide he was going to be courageous? Not really. Having learned about the power of thought, he could see that feeling like a victim was coming from his thinking, and he cut right through it. With this clarity, he then saw that helping Bill was the right thing to do, and he felt empowered to act. He also had a flow of thoughts about how to do it appropriately in the right feeling.

Leaders often look courageous because they take action at times without permission or when there is a risk. Look more closely and you will see that courage is only required when you have fear. When you recognize that you are feeling your thinking and not your circumstances, your mind clears and your fear subsides. A mind free of insecure thinking has clarity, perspective, insight, and humanity present in the moment.

Without worry, fear, or other thinking that can bog you down, the natural movement of your mind will help you see the obvious and you will find yourself acting with good judgment and common sense. This is leadership from within.

Great Leaders Bring Out the Best in Others

If you see the innate capacity for leadership built into your own core, chances are that you also see this innate capacity in others.

If you are in a leadership role with others, you can lead them toward synergy and high performance by engaging and supporting their innate leadership. To us, this is a significant role for any leader. It is humane and effective, and creates an environment in which people tend to thrive.

One executive quickly caught on to this dynamic just in time for a huge implementation he was responsible for:

Terry was referred to us because a number of complaints about him began flowing into HR. He was the Senior Vice

President in a Fortune 25 company who had the habit of getting angry and publicly chastising people when they failed to meet their commitments.

Although he had a big heart and was well liked by many, Terry's forceful style could be hard to stomach. He took pride in mentoring those who he considered worthy but felt justified in his outbursts toward those who didn't deliver as he expected.

When we began working with Terry, he struggled with the fact that he was feeling his own thinking. Because his feelings were so strong, he couldn't believe they were coming from his own mind. He was confident he was right.

"I know my feelings may be too strong for some to deal with," he told us, "but I want strong people around me. If I am not afraid of being really clear with folks and they can take it, then I know they are up to the job."

"Do you think being able to handle your strong feelings is the best measure of someone's ability to perform?" we asked him.

"Isn't it an important factor in leadership?" he asked.

"Maybe not. There is something more powerful in everyone's mind that is more central," we responded.

Terry reflected on this and responded, "I know there is, but sometimes I just run out of patience with people who are not that smart or capable."

As we discussed the matter, Terry had a hard time considering that his indignant and frustrated feelings were not coming from the situation. We had to address this before we could talk about how to bring out the innate wisdom in his people across the board.

"Are you telling me I shouldn't be frustrated with people who are not up to speed?" he asked at one point.

"We don't prescribe that anyone should or shouldn't feel any certain feeling at any time. We just point out how the operating system in the mind works. If you are emotionally upset, your mind is not as open or insightful as it can be. Your intelligence is limited to only the thinking making you upset at that moment. With that thinking, you won't see the situation with wisdom or have the opportunity to bring out the best in the other person. Don't you see that you end up behaving badly and regret it when you act from these feelings?"

The logic was sound, but it was hard for Terry to wrestle with what we were saying. He had been so used to justifying his feelings and acting on them. In time, the penny dropped, and he realized that his frustration was coming from his thinking when he was in an unbalanced state. "I have felt angry and justified my whole career when people didn't perform. This may be hard to give up," he said.

"Maybe," we responded. "It depends on how deeply you realize that those upset feelings are just your thoughts playing out in your feelings."

Soon after those insights settled in for him, we asked, "Aren't you clearer and more generous with people when you aren't reacting to things? Aren't you able to see the best in people and work to encourage their learning when you see them and their situations in perspective?"

"Sure."

"Can you see that there is an innate intelligence in you that enables that perspective and encouragement when your mind is open and relaxed?"

"Sure," he said again.

We were then able to make a crucial distinction for Terry. "People have varying degrees of what we ordinarily think of as intelligence, and people have different ways of being intelligent, yet behind that mental intelligence is something universal—an innate ability to be clear, thoughtful, insightful, and full of creative energy to see what is needed and to get things done."

It took a bit of conversation with lots of examples, but Terry did see the simplicity of the point we were making. Terry then reported a very interesting insight. "I always trusted the innate capacity in my strong people, but I didn't see it in anyone else. I didn't realize how much I was missing."

Terry realized that the wisdom and insight coming through him when in balance was a universal gift and not a reflection of his personal intelligence. He also realized the power his team would have if they all learned to see it as well.

This insight couldn't have come soon enough.

Terry and his team were tasked with leading a massive transformation process within the company: to change all the IT and business processes. He asked us to help infuse what he had learned throughout his team and to the rest of his functions. The results they achieved were remarkable. They completed the two-year project on time and on budget—a rare accomplishment for so complicated a change. Terry credited a good deal of the success to his team's knowledge of how the mind works.

"At every leadership team meeting," Terry told us afterwards, "we spent whatever time was needed checking in on how everyone and their teams were doing mentally. We knew that if everyone stayed clear and insightful, we could achieve our goals. We have never before completed a project of this size without running over. Our understanding saved us from spinning our wheels and wasting a huge amount of time and money."

When Terry realized that everyone is more likely to be wise and productive when they are balanced, attending to everyone's balance and well-being became a high priority.

There are many skills that a leader must have to succeed, but beneath those learned skills are fundamental capabilities that can be found in everyone. These qualities do not require effort or specific circumstances to come forward. They flow through you from your core when you are balanced. When you are in balance, your wisdom can show up fully, and from there, leadership is natural.

In Summary:

- Leadership is an innate capacity in all people.
- When you are at home or in balance, the main qualities of leadership rise to the surface effortlessly.
- Good leadership brings out the innate leadership in others.

A New Vision

We are not human beings having a spiritual experience.
We are spiritual beings having a human experience.

~ Pierre Teilhard de Chardin

It's not every day that a gift like insight principles falls into our laps.

We are very grateful to have come across what we have shared with you in this book. It has enabled life-changing shifts for all three of us. Though we still have our egos and our moods, they don't dominate our lives. We are comfortable being ourselves, and as our understanding deepens, we have more inner peace, inspiration to serve our clients, and the joy and energy with which to do so.

Everyone can have all this.

When the invisible facts of life are seen with new clarity, your life becomes simpler and humanity as a whole can evolve to new levels of well-being and creativity. This has happened in physics, medicine, aerodynamics, and many other fields. We are confident that what Sydney Banks saw will do the same for our understanding of the human mind.

We hope we have given you a clearer window into the innate wisdom, health, and goodness designed into the core of your mind. Too many live with unnecessary mental stress and suffering without realizing the spiritual intelligence residing within. If they only knew where to look! What a relief it is to realize that your default settings bring you to clarity, perspective, insight, and the embodiment of the best of humanity.

True as it is, most do not yet realize the inside→out nature of reality. We are constantly bombarded with messages that we are victims of our circumstances and that our happiness resides in having things or getting better and better circumstances. No lasting contentment or satisfaction lies in this direction. Due to this misunderstanding, crime, hate, war, and violence continue.

As more people realize the inside→out nature of human life, relationships, marriages, parenting, teamwork, and organizations can become places of greater health and service.

Imagine a world that functions this way. We do, which is why we spend all of our working lives sharing insight principles.

We trust that there is a natural evolution toward an effective global community infused with mental clarity and common sense, insight and compassion. Humanity can, and is designed to, evolve out of the problems it keeps recycling from one generation to the next. We believe that what we point to in this book can greatly accelerate this evolution.

These outcomes are possible. Not theoretically possible in some long distant future, but right now—this moment.

A true understanding of our human nature points us in this direction.

Thanks for being on the journey with us.

About Sydney Banks

As we mentioned in the introduction, none of what you have read would have been possible without Syd Banks. In 1973, Sydney Banks, a welder living in Canada who had emigrated from Scotland as a young man, had a profound enlightenment experience. He uncovered three principles that governed and explained the human experience, resulting in a paradigm shift in the understanding of who we are and why we do what we do.

Syd was an ordinary man, struggling like most people to make a living, care for his family, and be happy. He did not study or read spiritual or psychological literature, and was not searching for the meaning of life. He often said, "Why this happened to me, I'll never know."

From these humble beginnings, Syd became a world-renowned teacher and author. For more than forty years after his experience, he dedicated his life to alleviating human suffering.

Through his selfless efforts, he changed the lives of thousands of people. Although he passed away in 2009, the understanding he shared is thriving and being shared with an ever-increasing range of countries, venues, and audiences, from prisons to schools, and from professional athletics to businesses.

He left behind a collection of books and recordings that provide direct access to his discoveries. More information can be found on his website: http://sydneybanks.org/.

ABOUT US

Ken Manning, PhD

Ken has been interested in finding simple solutions to help people be at their best for as long as he can remember. He pursued three degrees in psychology from Brown University, Lesley College, and the University of Massachusetts at Amherst. He practiced as a clinical psychologist for twenty years.

In parallel to his career in psychology, Ken also has a strong background in business, including roles in various startups as national sales manager, director of marketing, and advisory board member. He cofounded, with his son-in-law, a successful software development company, which he still leads.

In 1999, he began innovating ways to bring insight principles into the corporate world and joined with partner Robin Charbit to form their company, Insight Principles.

Ken has been married for thirty years, has two stepdaughters, a son, and five grandchildren. He plays the piano, loves the outdoors and all kinds of sports and exercise, travel, photography, woodworking, and spending time with family and friends.

Robin Charbit

Robin began his career as a chemical engineer with Exxon in 1981 (having received his education at Sheffield University in the UK), and eventually led one of Exxon's international plastics businesses. He joined Arthur D. Little in 1992, first in Europe and ultimately in Boston, where he led and managed the North America Chemicals Practice.

With a colleague, Charlie Keifer, he left the more classical consulting world and founded Insight Management Partners to bring an understanding of how the mind works into business. He then met Ken Manning, and they joined forces to create Insight Principles.

Robin was born in the UK to French parents and met his Belgian wife, Sabine, in Switzerland. They now live in Boston with their three soccer-crazed children. When time permits, Robin enjoys all things mechanical (cars, woodworking, home projects) and is an avid cinemaphile.

Sandra Krot

Sandy's vision is to make the workplace a setting for creative performance as well as the elevation of the human spirit. After graduating from Bates College and the University of New Haven Graduate School, she began her career as a mental health counselor. She founded and served as Executive Director of one the first principle-based programs in the US, located in Tampa, Florida.

In 2000, she had her first opportunity to take a principle-based understanding of the mind to business. This led her in a new direction, and she joined Insight Principles in 2010.

Sandy shares her life with her partner, Peter Remick, and together they built their net-zero-energy home in rural Washington. They get out into the awesome Pacific Northwest wilderness as often as they can, sea kayaking, backpacking, and hiking with their dog.

SOURCES CITED

Banks, Sydney. *The Enlightened Gardener*. Alberta, Canada: Lone Pine, 2001.

Banks, Sydney. *The Enlightened Gardener Revisited*. Alberta, Canada: Lone Pine, 2005.

Banks, Sydney. *In Quest of the Pearl*. Alberta, Canada: Lone Pine, 1989.

Banks, Sydney. *The Missing Link*. Alberta, Canada: Lone Pine, 1998.

Banks, Sydney. *Second Chance*. Tampa: Duval-Bibb, 1983.

Collins, Jim. *Good To Great. Why Some Companies Make the Leap ... And Others Don't*. New York: Harper Business, 2001.

Covey, Stephen. *The Seven Habits of Highly Effective People*. New York: Simon & Schuster, 1989.

Criminal Justice. Alberta, Canada: Lone Pine Publishing. Video no longer available.

Santos, Michael. www.michaelsantos.com

Stone, Douglas, Bruce Patton, and Sheila Heen. *Difficult Conversations: How to Discuss What Matters Most*. New York: Penguin Books, 1999.

Made in the USA
Monee, IL
16 January 2020